TO KNOW A WARRIOR

A layman's defense of
Christian martial arts training and combat

By

Chuck Cobb

1

To Know a Warrior: A layman's defense of Christian martial arts training and combat by Chuck Cobb
Copyright © 2008 by Chuck Cobb
All Rights Reserved.
ISBN: 1-59755-156-2

Published by: ADVANTAGE BOOKS™
                www.advbookstore.com

Unless otherwise noted, Scripture taken from the HOLY BIBLE, NEW INTERNATIONAL VERSION ®. Copyright © 1973, 1978, 1984 by the International Bible Society. Used by permission of Zondervan Publishing House. All rights reserved.

Images from Bible Picture Gallery, Christian Computer Art, England (except image in Chapter 14)

Library of Congress Control Number: 2008930352

Cover design by Pat Theriault

First Printing: July 2008
08 09 10 11 12 13 14   10 9 8 7 6 5 4 3 2 1
Printed in the United States of America

To those warriors who serve,
that people may live free

To Know A Warrior

Acknowledgements

Thanks first and foremost to my merciful Lord, who loves me unconditionally and inspired me to write this book. Thanks to my diminutive mom, who showed me that size does not make a person. Thanks to my loving dad, who taught me as a young boy: "Son, don't ever start a fight; but if you have to fight, make sure you are the one who finishes it." Thanks to my solid, big brother, who gave me plenty of opportunity to practice my father's advice and learn from it. Thanks to my sweet wife, who gave me the liberty to train and compete in martial arts and to write this book. A special thanks to my gracious editor, who met my schedule. Thanks to my faithful pastor, who helped me to understand the heart of a servant. Finally, thanks to my grand master, who trained and encouraged me to persevere, and set an example of a Christian warrior.

To Know A Warrior

Table of Contents

Praise be to the LORD my Rock, who trains my hands for war, my fingers for battle.

David, Son of Jesse

Foreword

This book is incomplete. Many of the points raised herein demand elaboration. Yet with thousands of tomes already written, the main object of this brief treatise sustains discussion, study, and even worship.

However, the perspective presented herein is unique, although it is not original. It is simply a current look at a few small pieces of a colossal mosaic. But they are pieces of the puzzle that help bring the whole picture into view; links between pieces that aid in a better understanding of a complex world and its creator.

The violence in this world demands attention. One of the purposes of this book is to promote discussion; not discussion which results in idol conversation, but discussion that leads to action. The value of communication in promoting peace cannot be overemphasized. However, there can be no peace without liberty, including the liberty to engage in vice.

For peace without liberty is oppression, just as love cannot exist without free will. Peace without the means to maintain it is not sustainable in a world saturated with a propensity for violence. Until that root nature is changed, the virtues of peace, liberty, and love can only be assured by those who desire them the most.

David triumphs over Goliath

Introduction

The modern Christian church has failed in teaching an important attribute of God. The Bible tells us in Exodus 15:3 that "the LORD is a warrior." Yet every Sunday, the passive harmony of an old hymn tells the Christian soldier to march onward—in hollow rhetoric. From Genesis 14:14, where Abram "called out the 318 trained men" to rescue Lot from captivity, through Revelation 19:11, where Jesus Christ who "wages war in righteousness" returns on a white horse to do battle, the Holy Bible is filled with the stories of battles and wars and victories for God. Romans 15:4 tells us, "Everything that was written in the past was written to teach us." Two key themes therein are the mental and spiritual preparation necessary to live peacefully in a world filled with conflict. The physical aspect is an overlooked, but nevertheless important, component. With the objective to develop the whole student, Christian martial arts training is an appropriate and vital curriculum to teach a deep and practical understanding of the nature of God and Christian life.

The Bible says that David was a man after God's heart. As a boy, too young for battle, he visited his brothers on the front lines of the war against the Philistines. Seeing the Israelite army taunted by Goliath, he was filled with a righteous indignation to the point of entering the battle.

Outfitted by the soldiers with the armor of King Saul, David quickly realized he had lost his edge. Recognizing the advantage of agility, he shed the heavy armor and left the king's sword behind. David had a spirit of self-confidence, bolstered by his faith, which led to a mighty triumph for the Army of God. Although the Bible is not specific, it is fair to infer that David learned from his family and his community how to use a rock and sling for the defense of his flock and the nation of Israel. The shepherd boy David grew to become a great king and a mighty warrior for God.[1]

Teachers and preachers for generations have used the tale of the battle between David and Goliath in numerous sermons. This story encourages the faithful, as well as the weak in faith, to accomplish the insurmountable and to overcome great obstacles. It is frequently used as an allegory to teach countless other real and valuable lessons. But how many in the Christian faith of our current generation take the practical lesson of this story and use it to teach people the virtuous application of martial arts and combat? Ecclesiastes 3:1-8 says, "There is a time for everything...There is a time for war and a time for peace." A Christian must be active through both. Jesus Christ told the disciples to get a sword (Luke 22:36). It is reasonable to assume that He expected them to know how and when to use it. Christian martial arts training helps the believer better understand the warrior heart of God.

Introduction

An organic martial artist

Christian Martial Arts Defined

To understand why martial arts training is needed in the Christian church (the Church), it is important that church leaders and adherents have a clear understanding of the definition of Christian martial arts in the context of this apologetic. As commonly understood in contemporary culture, a martial art is a system in which a person is trained to fight using only the hands and feet, and is generally associated with Eastern or Asian cultures. Eastern-style martial arts are sometimes referred to as "traditional" martial arts, and usually include cryptic movement patterns commonly known as kata (as in karate), poomsae (as in taekwondo[1]), or simply as forms. Most traditional martial arts systems are not limited to the physical training, but also include mental and spiritual training of the person as key components of the curriculum. The physical and psychological training together defines the martial art.

In fact, other forms of hand-to-hand combat training technically qualify as martial arts, but are not typically recognized as such by most people. Martial arts are not usually equated with styles of fighting that have become widely accepted as a sport. However, the combat sports are not without their share of psychological training to some degree, and it is a critical component at a highly competitive level. Therefore, with both physical and psychological training, combat sports also meet the loose definition of a martial art. Using the fine arts as an analogy, there are as many different types of martial arts as there are types of music. There is classical, opera, pop, polka, hyang-ak,[2] gagaku,[3] gospel, and numerous other styles of music. Similarly, there is boxing, Greco-Roman wrestling, judo, jujutsu, karate, taekwondo, and numerous other styles of martial art. The inspirations, foundations, variations, and purposes for playing music or fighting are similarly complex.

Advanced martial arts usually include training with certain handheld weapons such as a sword or even ordinary items such as a cane or walking stick. Fencing, archery, and shooting (small arms) are personal-weapon disciplines currently practiced as sports. A long look back at history shows that martial art is actually the original rampart of survival, self-defense, and military training in preparation for war. Of course, in modern war, technology has rendered the hand and sword into a good example for the definition of obsolete. It is often said that only a fool would bring a knife to a gunfight.

But the concept of battle transcends invention. To paraphrase a respected Christian teacher of the author, an inorganic, material thing should be pursued at its most technologically advanced state while an organic, natural thing should always be pursued at its purest and most original state.[4] Learning to use the hands and feet for combat represents this thought in context. From an organic perspective then, for those moved by good conscience, martial art is a system wherein a person is trained to recognize danger and defend one's self or others against attack, using only the hands and feet, or weapons as available and necessary for the magnitude of the situation. The definition of Christian martial arts used herein becomes: Any of the physical, martial or fight training disciplines that include and emphasize a Biblically sound basis for the mental and spiritual development of the student.

Most importantly, the Christian martial artist must understand when the use of force is appropriate. The primary objectives of Christian martial arts training are to physically, mentally, and spiritually develop the whole student, to train persons for spiritual battle, and to know God. If God wants us to know Him and be like Him, then for Christians to ignore martial arts training is to ignore one of the most visible, and perhaps the most misunderstood, attributes of God throughout history.

Bandits in ambush

The Parable of the Samaritan Warrior

To pursue the concept of Christian martial arts, the question comes up: How can a Christian justify being involved in martial arts training? The answer is found in an alternative question: When is combat of any nature appropriate? Borrowing a teaching method from the Master, consider the parable of the Samaritan warrior.

A priest who had finished his work late one evening began his walk toward home. Passing through the business district, he noticed a young woman surrounded by a group of men. The lady was modestly dressed and fear was evident on her face. The priest thought the scene was a bit unusual. But there were three large men, surly and dour, and the priest, being a pacifist, was intimidated by their appearance. He pretended not to see them as he quickened his pace and hurried home to the security of his locked door. Not long afterward, a Pharisee followed along the same route and saw the group of men pushing and pulling the young lady along on the other side of the street. The woman was obviously struggling to get away, but the Pharisee observed that the woman was a Canaanite, and so was not concerned for her safety. About that time, a Samaritan businessman who was locking the door to his store saw the men turn into an alley with the obviously distressed young woman under their control. The Samaritan was a trained warrior, not afraid of any man, and he immediately recognized the peril of the innocent victim. By the time he rounded the corner, the men had thrown the woman to the ground and begun their assault. Confronted by the boldness of the Samaritan, two of the attackers immediately fled. However, the largest of the men was a determined criminal, but failed to recognize his own peril in the Samaritan warrior. After the thug was soundly defeated, he fled at his first opportunity to escape the punishment he was receiving at the hands of the defender of the innocent. Who among these showed the love of the Father for his children?

Perhaps the defense of others is the best example of when it is appropriate to use force. A Christian who would dispute this concept would be "kicking against the goads", for the Bible makes it clear that God is a defender of the innocent. James, the brother of Jesus, said, "Religion that God our Father accepts as pure and faultless is this: to look after widows and orphans in their distress, and to keep oneself from being polluted by the world" (James 1:27). Defending the helpless is one of the best examples of charity. Jesus himself said, "Greater love has no one than this, that he would lay down his life for his friends." A righteous warrior takes this charity to another level, in that he is willing to put his life at risk for someone he may not even know.

There are circumstances for which combat is an appropriate action to prevent injustice. The issue is one of propriety. Christian philosophy is a critical foundation for the righteous warrior. In order to recognize when martial arts are properly applied, the warrior must be trained in moral teachings such as honor, integrity, and most importantly, love. These virtues and more are the guiding principles for the physical aspects of Christian martial arts. To enter battle requires courage, but to enter battle without training is foolish.

The appropriate time to learn the skills necessary to defend others is before those skills are required. However, the chances of actually having to fight are relatively rare in a civilized society, and one may live and die without a physical encounter. But there is a spiritual element to our world, and in it there are those who are motivated by evil intent. Ephesians 6:11-12 says, "Put on the full armor of God so that you may take your stand against the devil's schemes. For our struggle is not against flesh and blood, but against the rulers, against the authorities, against the powers of this dark world and against the spiritual forces of evil in the heavenly realms." The benefit of the ability to enter a fight with the confidence that comes from training directly translates to the struggles most people encounter along the road of life; physical, psychological, or spiritual.

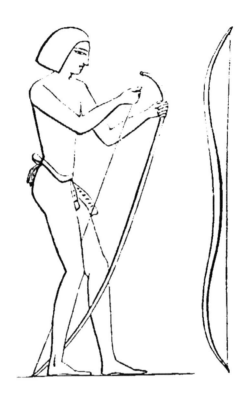

Egyptian archery student

Martial Training
in the
Bible

The Bible is relatively quiet about actual martial or military training, but it is not completely silent about the topic. The fact that stories of wars and battles are so prevalent therein allows the reader to assume that some type of training occurred, although no specific instructions or commands are emphasized. The first of few references to martial training in the Bible occurs in Genesis 14. Abram (later to be called Abraham) was living in an area where several kings were at war. The conquering king kidnapped Abram's relative, Lot, and all of Lot's family, and carried them into captivity. Genesis 14:14 states that when Abram heard of Lot's capture, he "called out" the "trained" men of his household. They pursued the marauders, routed them in a nighttime raid, and rescued Lot and his family. The King James Version (KJV) of the Bible says that Abram "armed his trained servants." A lexical review of this passage is of interest.

The Hebrew word for "trained" used in Genesis 14:14 is *chaniyk* (phonetically pronounced "kaw-neek") and only occurs here in the entire Bible. The Hebrew Lexicon defines the word as "properly initiated; hence skilled, of tried fidelity."[1] Also of interest in this passage is the Hebrew word *ruwq* (phonetically pronounced "rook"), which is translated in the KJV Bible as "armed"; however, the New International Version (NIV) of the Bible translates the word as "called out." The Hebrew Lexicon defines this word as "to pour one self out, to be poured out, to be emptied, whence…empty", but out of 19 occurrences in the KJV Bible, ruwq is only translated as "armed" in this one verse.[2] It appears clear from the context that Abram's men were prepared for battle; however, the form of the combat is not so clear. Incidentally, certain styles of martial arts are known as "the way of the empty hand."[3] One thing is for certain: if Abram's men were not empty handed, they were armed only with javelins or bows or swords, at best. Although a scholastic defense of the martial arts training implied in this passage of Scripture is beyond the scope of this study and the expertise of the author, the association is intriguing.

In the majority of the Old Testament, skill with arms appears to be taken for granted, as evidenced by King Saul's soldiers, who outfitted David in the king's armor and expected him to battle Goliath thus armed. Yet David sings praise to God who "trains my hands for battle; my arms can bend a bow of bronze" (II Samuel 22:35, Psalm 18:34). Here again, a lexical review is of interest. In the KJV Bible these passages begin, "He teacheth my hand for war…"

The Hebrew word *yarah* (phonetically pronounced "yaw-raw") is translated "teacheth" here and is defined in the Hebrew Lexicon as "to cast...an arrow ...an archer." *Yarah* is used 84 times in the KJV Bible in various contexts, from teaching the commandments of God (Exodus 24:12) to archers shooting arrows from a wall (II Samuel 11:24).[4] Here is a direct and profound association in the Bible between training and actual implements of war. Certainly there were many things that the teachers of the day cast forth like arrows for the students to learn; however, it is fair to assume that at least some of God's chosen people were taught to fight, using only their hands, slings, swords, and bows.

In one story, God is emphatic about martial training. He reveals His divine purpose to deliver those oppressed by sin in the brief span of the life of Othniel, faithful Caleb's little brother. Othniel was untested when he entered the battle for God. The power of the Living Word is revealed in God's management of the nations. God's faithfulness in Scripture speaks for itself:

> These are the nations the LORD left to test all those Israelites who had not experienced any of the wars in Canaan (he did this only to teach warfare to the descendants of the Israelites who had not had previous battle experience): the five rulers of the Philistines, all the Canaanites, the Sidonians... Perrizites, Hivites, and Jebusites. [The Israelites] took their daughters in marriage and gave their own daughters in marriage to their

sons, and they served their gods…The anger of the LORD burned…so he sold them into the hands of Cushan-Rishathaim king of Aram Naharaim, to whom they were subject for eight years…He raised up for them a deliverer, Othniel son of Kenaz, Caleb's younger brother, who saved them. The spirit of the LORD came upon him, so that he became Israel's judge and went to war. The LORD gave [the king] into the hands of Othniel, who overpowered him. So the land had peace for forty years, until Othniel son of Kenaz died [sic]. (Judges 3:1-11)

King David and his warriors in worship

The Sound of the Shofar

Wars and struggles occur throughout the Bible, with relatively few specific references to martial training beyond those noted. But the specific references to warriors of God are numerous. The warriors of God were called to battle at the sound of the shofar. The shofar is a trumpet made of a ram's horn. Joshua marched around Jericho for six days, with the priests of God blowing the shofar as they led the ark of the God. "The armed men went ahead of them and the rear guard followed the ark of the LORD, while the trumpets kept sounding" (Joshua 6:13b). On the seventh day, after a "long blast on the trumpet," the warriors gave their faithful "war cry" and the walls of Jericho fell. In First Corinthians 14:8, the Apostle Paul asks, "If the trumpet does not sound a clear call, who will get ready for battle?" Like the spiritual warrior Paul, the Christian warriors of today hear the sound of the shofar in their hearts. The duty of the Church is to help these brave men and women fulfill the purpose and call of God in their lives.

Before one can understand the warrior nature of God, it is first necessary to distinguish between soldiers and warriors. Colonel Kim Young Oak, a decorated, Korean-American warrior and veteran of World War II and the Korean War explains the difference:

Japan was a warrior nation. Korea was a scholar nation. Therefore, the warrior class, that is to say, the samurai, became the prime movers of society and eventually fulfilled the roll of scholar as well. On the other hand, in the Chosun [Korea] there was a very clear separation between the scholar and the soldier wherein even with the Yangban class those associated with military affairs were considered soldiers and not warriors. What then is the distinction between soldier and warrior? Warriors are autonomously armed people while soldiers are heteronomously armed people. The warrior chooses to carry a sword because he is skilled in its use. In the case of a soldier, he is consigned a sword by the authority of the state, regardless of his skill or [intention] of its use…While the warrior's sword serves its master, the soldier's individual existence is one of servitude to the sword. He does not employ the sword, it employs him…Martial arts emanates from warriors. What soldiers produce is not martial art but military science [sic].[1]

A soldier is an otherwise ordinary person who has been conscripted into service; in contrast, a warrior is a man (or woman) who is not afraid to fight because of the attitude within his (or her) heart. The Bible generally supports this description. As told in First Samuel 10 through 14, the Israelite people sinned against God and asked for a king, and the prophet Samuel anointed the tall and handsome

Saul. King Saul was accompanied by "valiant men[2] whose hearts God had touched." But when the City of Jabesh came under siege by the Ammonites, Saul conscripted 330,000 men under threat of penalty and pressed them into battle, even though they were armed only with "plowshares, mattocks, axes, and sickles." After the victory handed to them by God, Saul chose 3,000 men and sent the remainder home. Facing another battle against an army of Philistines, the Israelites were "quaking with fear...and began to scatter," and within a few days, Saul was down to about 600 men. First Samuel 14:52 says, "All the days of Saul there was bitter war with the Philistines, and whenever Saul saw a mighty or brave man, he took him into his service." Although some of Saul's men were surely warriors, the majority appear to be soldiers drafted into his army. In this entire passage, the men were described as "men of Israel" and "troops," but never as "warriors."

In contrast, in First Samuel 16, a servant said to Saul, "I have seen a son of Jesse...a brave man and a warrior...and the LORD is with him," and so the boy David was introduced to the king. Previously God had told Samuel to anoint one of Jesse's sons and said, "Do not consider his appearance or his height...The LORD does not look at the things man looks at. Man looks at the outward appearance, but the LORD looks at the heart." Consider what God said in Psalm 89:19-20, "I have bestowed strength on a warrior; I have exalted a young man from among the people. I have found David my servant; with my sacred oil I have anointed him." Here, He anoints a young warrior as king "in the presence of his brothers, and from that day on the Spirit of the LORD came upon David in power" (I Samuel 16:13). Samuel previously told Saul that God was looking for "a man after his own heart" (I Samuel 13:14). David was a man after God's heart because he had the heart of a warrior and the heart of a servant. A warrior is the ultimate servant because he is willing to lay down his life for his master.

First Chronicles 12:38 tells us that David had a volunteer army, "fighting men who volunteered to serve in the ranks." The last two chapters of Second Samuel are focused on David's warriors. Although it was a sin for David to count them, within Israel and Judah there were 1.4 million "fighting men…who could handle a sword," showing that the warriors were, at least, not uncommon. The warriors of David are recounted again in First Chronicles 11 and 12. Here the Bible speaks most clearly:

> These were the chiefs of David's mighty men—they, together with all Israel, gave his kingship strong support to extend it over the whole land, as the LORD had promised—this is the list of David's mighty men…Jashobeam, a Hacmonite, was chief of the officers; he raised his spear against three hundred men, whom he killed in one encounter…Next to him was Eleazar, son of Dodai the Ahohite…He was with David…and [they] struck the Philistines down, and the LORD brought about a great victory…Benaiah son of Jehoiada was a valiant fighter from Kabzeel, who performed great exploits…The mighty men were:

[among others, 46 are listed by name]…These were the men who came to David at Ziklag…they were among the warriors who helped him in battle; they were armed with bows and were able to shoot arrows or to sling stones right-handed or left-handed…Some Gadites defected to David at his stronghold in the desert. They were brave warriors, ready for battle and able to handle the shield and spear. Their faces were the faces of lions, and they were as swift as gazelles on the mountains…These Gadites were army commanders; the least was a match for a hundred, and the greatest was a match for a thousand…Other Benjamites and some men from Judah also came to David in his stronghold…Then the Spirit [of God] came upon Amasai…and he said: "We are yours, O David! We are with you, O son of Jesse! Success, success to you, and success to those who help you, for your God will help you."…all of them were brave warriors, and they were commanders in his army. Day after day men came to help David, until he had a great army, like the army of God.

Warriors hold a special place in the Holy Bible, in God's heart, and in God's economy. God showed His favoritism to the fighting men of Moses in Numbers 31:25-30 when He reduced the tribute to the LORD of the veterans ten times less than the tribute required of the remainder of the Israelites. The warrior is like Christ, the ultimate servant, in that he is, by nature of his identity, willing to put his life at risk to conduct his occupation, and God rewards him for it. (So should a nation.)

From a worldly perspective, the warrior is often perceived to be intent on domination at any expense in order to gain power and control. In contrast, the motivation of the Christian warrior is to defend the innocent from the aggressive warrior or soldier under evil command. These interdictions are always defensive in nature; however, this position is not to be confused with that of a pacifist, who would sit back and allow innocents to be abused and killed before taking up arms in defense of others. Nor is it to be confused with a strategic offensive launched by the righteous warrior to win the fight.

The Christian martial artist hears and understands the warrior's call. He knows how to control the power God has given him in the strength of the hands and feet and skill with other weapons, and when to use that strength and skill in a warrior's service to the innocent. In this ministry, the Christian warrior is sustained, protected, and blessed by the Almighty God.

The Sound of the Shofar

Samson fights a lion

Warriors of the Faith

Christian teachers often refer to the eleventh chapter of Hebrews when discussing the "heroes of the faith." Many of those named were warriors, "who through faith conquered kingdoms, <u>administered justice</u> [emphasis added], and gained what was promised; who shut the mouths of lions, quenched the fury of the flames, and escaped the edge of the sword; whose weakness was turned to strength; and who became powerful in battle and routed foreign armies." The unknown writer of the Book of Hebrews stated that he did "not have time to tell about" all of these faithful, but a quick review of a select few will prove insightful to further understand the warrior heart of God.

Gideon

Because of their sins, the Israelites were dominated and overrun by the Midianites for seven years. After they cried out to God, an unnamed prophet reminded the Israelites what the LORD had done for them in Egypt and who the LORD was. Then the "angel of the LORD appeared to Gideon" and said, "The LORD is with you, mighty warrior...Go in the strength you have and save Israel out of Midian's hand. Am I not sending you?" Gideon was skeptical because he considered himself the "least" of his family and his clan as the "weakest in Manasseh," and he asked the angel for a sign. Because his request was granted, Gideon prepared a young goat and unleavened bread, which were consumed with fire that flared from a rock. At the realization that he had seen the likeness of God in person, Gideon feared for his life. But God spoke to him and said, "Peace! Do not be afraid. You are not going to die." Providentially, Gideon named the altar that he built there "the LORD is Peace." The KJV Bible uses the transliteration "Jehovah-shalom," one of the popular compound names used in the Bible to reveal the character of God.[1] Gideon went on to sound the shofar and called the Israelites to arms. But too many responded for God to get the glory for the defeat, so God winnowed Gideon's army down to 300 men. God used Gideon and this tiny army to rout the Midianites and usher in 40 years of peace (Judges 6 through 8).

Barak

Barak is listed after Gideon in Hebrews, but Barak preceded Gideon in the Old Testament. In fact, the reference to Barak leads us to Deborah, who was the leader of the Israelites after twenty years of oppression by Sisera, the commander of the army of the Canaanites. Deborah ordered Barak to prepare for battle against Sisera, but Barak refused unless Deborah accompanied him. Deborah agreed, but prophesied that the honor of the victory would not go to Barak, "for the LORD will hand Sisera over to a woman." When Sisera heard of Barak's army, he assembled his "nine hundred iron chariots," and prepared for battle. Deborah ordered Barak to attack, and Sisera was forced to abandon his chariot and flee. All of the Canaanite army was slaughtered, except Sisera, who hid in the tent of Jael, the wife of a man in a clan with whom Sisera's king was on friendly terms. But the refuge was not secure, and while Sisera slept, Jael drove a tent peg through his temple with a hammer. The Israelites went on to destroy the king of the Canaanites (Judges 4). Deborah and Barak sang on that day:

> When the princes in Israel take the lead,
> When the people willingly offer themselves --
> Praise the LORD.

> Hear this, you kings! Listen, you rulers! I will sing to the LORD, I will sing...

> When they chose new gods, war came to the city gates, and not a shield or spear was seen among forty thousand in Israel.

> My heart is with Israel's princes, with the willing volunteers among the people.
> Praise the LORD!...

> Consider the voice of the singers at the watering places. They recite the righteous acts of the LORD, the righteous acts of the warriors in Israel...

The people of the LORD came to me with the mighty. Some came from Ephraim…

Benjamin was with the people who followed you. From Makir captains came down, from Zebulun those who bear a commander's staff.

The princes of Issachar were with Deborah; yes, Issachar was with Barak, rushing after him into the valley. In the districts of Reuben there was much searching of heart. Why did you stay among the campfires, to hear the whistling for the flocks?…

Gilead stayed beyond the Jordan. And Dan, why did he linger by the ships? Asher remained on the coast and stayed in his coves.
The people of Zebulon risked their very lives;
So did Naphtali on the heights of the field.

Kings came, they fought; The kings of Canaan fought at Taanach by the waters of Meggido [Armageddon]…

From the heavens the stars fought, From their courses they fought against Sisera… "Curse Meroz" said the angel of the LORD. "Curse its people bitterly, because they did not come to help the LORD, to help the LORD against the mighty." Most blessed of women be Jael…

Most blessed of tent dwelling women…
She struck Sisera, she crushed his head…
At her feet he sank. There he fell dead…
So may all your enemies perish, O LORD!
But may they who love you be like the sun when
it rises in its strength. (Judges 5)

And so began forty years of peace in the land, thanks to the martial service of the women, especially Deborah and Jael, who received special honor, and the men, including Barak and the warriors who volunteered to fight on the behalf of God's people. Two other points from this song are notable: The fighting of the stars from heaven reflects the element of spiritual warfare that occurred simultaneously with this battle; and the angel of God cursed those who refused to serve in spite of the convictions in their hearts.

Samson

No review of biblical warriors would be complete without consideration of Samson, the most famous, non-mythical strong man in the history of the world. Samson was a colorful character whose life was marked by distinction, sin, betrayal, comedic images, violence, and destiny. Dedicated to God before birth, Samson's legendary strength was associated with his long hair, and his divine purpose was to avenge the oppression of the Jews. As a young man, his life became entwined with the Philistines when he grieved his parents by seeking a wife from among their oppressors. Samson began his life of vengeance after he was betrayed by his betrothed and killed 30 Philistine men to pay off a ridiculous bet. On another occasion, he torched their fields with flame-bearing foxes and terrorized the Philistines. Frustrated with their inability to neutralize Samson, the Philistines pressured the Israelite men to control him. But Samson appeared to fear only his kinsmen, for he made the Israelites promise not to kill him if he surrendered to their treason. The Israelite men handed Samson over to the Philistines where he quickly regained his liberty when he slaughtered a thousand Philistines with the "jawbone of an ass." He called upon God in his thirst, and God provided a spring of water. But Samson was subject to the weakness of men, and he lusted for the infamous Delilah. Apart from understanding the power of the trap of sin, it is difficult to understand why Samson languished in her overt betrayals. He eventually divulged the secret to his strength, and Delilah called in the barbers. Weakened by his foolishness, Samson was blinded and chained in servitude. There he toiled, turning a gristmill in his mortal strength. Humiliated and forced to perform, Samson danced at the command of the Philistines. He was displayed in the temple, standing between two pillars during the Philistine festival. Subdued beyond recovery, Samson called out to God. By then his hair had grown long again, and as his super-human strength returned, Samson pushed down the columns, dying in the destruction of the Philistines (Judges 13 through 16).

So the question is: Why did the lust-filled Samson make Hebrew's list of the faithful? The bottom line is that, by the grace of God, the depth of a man's faith is not measured by the height of his sin. Nor is the breadth of his accomplishments measured by the extent of his failures. But the fruit identifies the tree (Galatians 5:22, Luke 3:9). The lessons from Samson's life are spiritual as well as corporal. God certainly showed His faithfulness to use dedicated Samson for His ultimate purpose, in spite of Samson's foolishness. Samson was an instrument that God used to avenge the suffering of the Israelites. In Samson's life, we see again God's jealousy for His chosen people and His love of liberty. God used Samson to rescue His people from the oppressive and worldly government of the Philistines.

There is another overlooked but critical lesson in Samson's life and death that is pertinent in light of contemporary events. It is important to note that in spite of Samson's obsession with the enemy, and his self-avenging ambition, he was not suicidal. Samson did not wish for death, and he ensured his own safety before submitting to the Israelite's treason. He clearly did not fear death at the hands of the Philistines. It was only in dire straits that he gave his life for the destruction of the enemy. Samson died in valor, serving God's purpose, for the benefit of his people.

Jephthah

The story of Jephthah is an ancient tragedy. Jephthah made Hebrew's list of the faithful, but the writer's lack of time may have been a convenient excuse to avoid the telling of a painful tale. With the Church in its infancy, the author may have known that this report was only suitable only for the mature of faith. The narrative is of interest to this study because Judges 11:1 says, "Jephthah the Gileadite was a mighty warrior."

Jephthah was also an illegitimate child, the son of Gilead and a prostitute. Ostracized by his brothers and excluded from his inheritance, he was forced to flee to another town in which to live. But when the Ammonites threatened Israel, the elders of Gilead called on Jephthah to lead them. As it turned out, Jephthah appeared to be a reasonable and educated man. He questioned why the elders asked for his assistance because they had driven him away, and made a solemn agreement with the men of Gilead that he would become their ruler should he prevail. After Jephthah took command, he tried to negotiate with the Ammonites and sent them a detailed history of the area of land under dispute. He challenged their claim to the land with facts, and when they ignored his message, "the Spirit of the LORD came upon him," and Jephthah attacked. As the gravity of the situation pressed upon him, it appears that his faith wavered and he tried to bargain with God, making a vow that would rend his heart: "If you give the Ammonites into my hands, whatever comes out of the door of my house to meet me when I return in triumph from the Ammonites will be the LORD's, and I will sacrifice it as a burnt offering" (Judges 11:30-31). It is within the realm of possibility that his goats had the run of the place, but when he returned home from defeating the Ammonites, his only child, a daughter, was the first out the door. Jephthah was devastated. Judges 11:39 indicates that he kept his vow to God. But the tragedy of Jephthah's story doesn't end there.

The men of Ephraim appeared to be jealous of his victory. They threatened to burn down his house, and insulted the heritage of the Gileadites. Fighting broke out within the tribe of Israel, and the Gileadites fought a bloody battle with the Ephraimites. At the ford of the Jordan, Jephthah cleverly distinguished the clans, and killed men according to their accents. Forty-two thousand Ephraimites were killed in this civil war between distant cousins (Judges 11 and 12).

Again the question: Why did Jephthah make it to the famous list of the Bible's faithful? Biblical scholars debate whether Jephthah was guilty of human sacrifice.[2] But the author of Hebrews and the faithful of today who know Jesus Christ, understand that His redemptive work was sufficient to cover even such an atrocity. Jephthah clearly understood the value of commitment and appears to have been a man of his word. These are worthy attributes, but hardly a measure of faith. The important lesson of faith begins in Jephthah's appeal to the Ammonites. He knew the Israelites had a legitimate claim to the land and that battle was not necessary. Jephthah was not perfect, far from it; but he knew about the hand of God in the Israelites history and he believed in God. Abraham believed in God, and his belief was "credited to him as righteousness" (Exodus 15:6). The same credit of righteousness is available to the imperfect believers of today.

David's loyal men fetch water from Bethlehem

Learning from the Warriors of God

Biblical exegesis uses typology to understand the New Testament revelation of Jesus Christ.[1] Typology is the study of Old Testament figures who possess certain characteristics that help the student learn about the nature and character of God. A review of some key Christ-types in the Old Testament provides important insight to understand God's attitude toward fighting.

Jacob

One of the earliest biblical examples of unarmed, hand-to-hand combat is recorded in Genesis 32:22-30. A patriarch of God's chosen people, Jacob was alone one night when he encountered a man with whom he wrestled until the break of dawn. Jacob was clearly a skilled and determined wrestler, for he grappled with God Himself and refused to submit, even after God wounded him by injuring his hip. That morning, God blessed Jacob for his perseverance and changed his name to Israel. Jacob went on to sire twelve sons, who became the twelve tribes of Israel. When Jacob was more than 147 years old, he gave his son Joseph, who was second in command over all of Egypt, "the ridge of land I took from the Amorites with my sword and my bow" (Genesis 48:22). The old wrestler went on to prophesy over his sons (Genesis 49). He cursed Simeon and Levi for killing men in anger (Genesis 34:26). For other sons, he foreshadowed battles and wars, peace and prosperity, slavery and justice. For Joseph, Jacob predicted "his bow remained steady, his strong arms stayed limber, because of the Mighty one of Jacob, because of the Shepherd, the Rock of Israel" (Genesis 49:24). And for Judah, Jacob described a messianic prophesy of the second coming of Jesus Christ, the "Lion of the Tribe of Judah" (Revelation 5:5):

> Judah, your brothers will praise you; your hand will be on the neck of your enemies; your father's sons will bow down to you.
>
> You are a lion's cub, O Judah; you return from the prey, my son, like a lioness—who dares to rouse him?
>
> The scepter will not depart from Judah, nor the rulers staff from between his feet, until he comes to whom it belongs, and the obedience of the nations is his. (Genesis 49:8-10)

Moses

The whole story of Moses and the Book of Exodus is a theological review of the nature of God and His purpose, with themes of God's presence, His attributes, and His redemption.[2] Moses was most likely familiar with martial arts training, having grown up in Egypt in the house of Pharaoh. He may have used the training inappropriately when he murdered the Egyptian for abusing the Hebrew slave (Exodus 2:11-12), but his motive was to defend the innocent. Without knowing, he was being led to a higher purpose. Moses fled into the desert, and later rescued a shepherdess from the disrespectful shepherds at the well (Exodus 2:17). God eventually used Moses to rescue the Jewish people from their oppression in Egypt. After the Passover, Moses led the Israelites out of Egypt, "armed for battle" (Exodus 13:18). God's presence was clearly visible in this story, and he performed spectacular miracles that all of the people could see. But even after God parted the Red Sea and destroyed Pharaoh's army, the Hebrew people were required to use their weapons in self-defense.

For us, the lessons are spiritual. The Amalekites (evil) attacked the Israelites (God's people), so Moses sent Joshua and his men out to fight them (resistance). Moses took the staff of God and held up his hands (an appeal to God for help[3]). As long as his hands were up, they were winning, and when they were down, they were losing. When his arms grew tired, he sat on a rock while Aaron and Hur held his hands up (support from others). Joshua defeated the Amalekites, and Moses built an altar there and named it "the LORD is my Banner." In the KJV, the altar is named "Jehovah-nissi," another one of the compound names of God. And Moses said, "the LORD will be at war with the Amalekites from generation to generation" (Exodus 17:8-16). And so evil continues to attack God's people today, and through Christian martial arts training, we learn to persevere in battle, to accept support from others, and to depend on God to win.

Joshua

Joshua is a great typological study because his very name means "the LORD saves," which is translated in Greek as "Jesus."[4] Before Moses called him Joshua, he was Hoshea, son of Nun. Hoshea means "salvation."[5] Joshua was Moses' closest and most trusted aid. He was one of the twelve men sent to spy on the land of Canaan. Joshua and the faithful Caleb were the only two who were not afraid to go up and take the land, in spite of the giants who reportedly lived there (Exodus 13:1-14:9). Before Moses died, God placed Joshua in charge of leading the Israelites and said to him, "Be strong and courageous, for you will bring the people into the land I promised them on oath, and I myself will be with you" (Deuteronomy 31:23). Because of their faith in God, Joshua and Caleb were the only two out of their whole generation who entered the Promised Land. Joshua led the people in the battle against Jericho, and breached their fortress with the trumpet (Joshua 6). He laid an ambush, defeated the king of Ai, and destroyed the city with his javelin (Joshua 8). Joshua marched with his army all night to rescue the Gibeonites from the five kings of the Amorites. He took the kings by surprise and God "hurled large hailstones down on them from the sky," killing more than the Israelites did with the sword. Joshua appealed to God, and the sun and the moon stood still for a whole day. "There has never been a day like it before or since, a day when the LORD listened to a man. Surely the

LORD was fighting for Israel" (Joshua 10:1-14). Joshua was credited as a military strategist and a statesman.[6] He was clearly a great warrior, and God fought alongside him.

David

David is one of the most important Christ-types in the Old Testament. David wrote, "Praise be to the LORD my Rock, who trains my hands for war, my fingers for battle. He is my loving God and my fortress, my stronghold and my deliverer..." (Psalm 144:1-2). By examining the heart of David, one can further understand the heart of God. However, it is important to note that David was not perfect, and the Christian warrior can learn lessons from the sin in David's life, as well. The following limited selection of Davidic attributes can help a person know about the warrior heart of God.

> **Loyalty**—The importance of loyalty needs emphasis in the church today, and David is an ideal example because he was one of the most loyal men in the Bible. His loyalty to Israel was shown in his willingness to enter the battle against Goliath, armed primarily with his faith in God. He was doggedly loyal to King Saul, whom he acknowledged as his master. David's loyalty to Saul was extraordinary, for he remained loyal even though Saul tried to kill him, and David refused to lift a sword against the King (I Samuel 24 through 26). David's loyalty was such that it inspired loyalty in others, and godly warriors

began to join him in the desert. David's wish was the command of his loyal men, and they risked their lives simply to bring him a drink of water from the well at Beth Shalom (I Chronicles 11:15-19). David was also loyal to Jonathan, son of Saul, with whom he demonstrated the love of a best friend. David's loyalty to Jonathan even transcended Jonathan's death, and after David became king, he searched the kingdom for Saul's family. He found Mephibosheth, son of Jonathan, seated him at the king's table, and restored to him the wealth of Saul (II Samuel 9). Samuel's prophecies were fulfilled when first the people of Judah, then the people of Israel, anointed him as their king and pledged their loyalty (II Samuel 2:4 and 5:3, respectively). Above all, David was loyal to God.

Compassion—David was a shepherd as a young boy and the experience followed him through life. As a mature warrior, he was protective of and compassionate to those around him. It is easy to understand that he would pursue the Amelekites, who kidnapped his family from Ziklag (I Samuel 30). But David also protected those for whom he owed no allegiance. While David and his band of men were hiding from Saul in the Desert of Maon, the servant of wealthy Nabal said that David was a "wall around us all the time" (I Samuel 24:16). David inquired of God, who assured him of victory in rescuing the people of Keilah from the Philistine army (I Samuel 23). King David ordered Saul's servants to serve the crippled Mephibosheth for the remainder of his days. Although David was a mighty warrior, he understood the heart of God; therefore, he was also a man of compassion. As a writer, David reflected the heart of God when he wrote the Psalms and he cried out, "Have mercy on me, O God, according to your unfailing love; according to your great compassion blot out my transgressions. Wash away all my iniquity and cleanse me from my sin" (Psalm 51:1). Judges 2:18b says, "…the LORD had compassion on them as they groaned under those who oppressed them and afflicted them." Compassion for the weak, the helpless, and the oppressed are motives for the Christian warrior. When he goes to their rescue, the Christian warrior suffers alongside them.

Patience—David was "only a boy" when he was anointed to be king and took on the giant in battle. Although he was clearly a warrior, it seems he was required to learn other more important attributes before he would realize his kingdom. After fleeing for his life, David was hiding from King Saul when he was protecting Nabal at Maon. David became enraged when Nabal refused his cordial request for supplies. He was preparing the assault when Nabal's wife, Abigail, intervened, and David learned one of the most important lessons for the Christian warrior. David understood clearly as he proclaimed to Abigail, "Praise be to the LORD, the God of Israel, who has sent you today to meet me. May you be blessed for your good judgment and for keeping me from bloodshed this day and <u>from avenging myself with my own hands</u>" [emphasis added] (I Samuel 25:32). Nabal died at the hand of God ten days later. David went on to spare the life of Saul on two occasions and refused to claim his kingdom. Even after Saul fell on his sword, David waited. "In the course of time, David inquired of the LORD....So David went up [to Hebron]...and there [the men of Judah] anointed David king over the house of Judah" (II Samuel 2:1-4). Eventually, the tribes of Israel and Judah assembled in Hebron and anointed David king over all Israel. He was thirty years old. More than likely, it was at least fifteen years, perhaps twenty, before he realized the promise of God. Even though God ordained David to be king, it is important to note that David did not take his kingdom by force, even though he commanded a great army. Proverbs 16:32 says, "Better is a patient man than a warrior; one who controls his temper than one who takes a city." Patience is a higher virtue for the Christian warrior to possess.

Integrity—David was a man after the heart of God, anointed as a child to become king of Israel, with a promise by God to always have an heir on the throne. Yet David's life example is one of utter humanity. When he was well established as king, he fell into lust with the beautiful Bathsheba and committed adultery. After she became pregnant, he tried to cover it up, and arranged a sabbatical for his faithful warrior servant, Uriah. Uriah refused to sleep with his wife while his comrades were at war, so David sent him to the front lines where he was killed in battle. David then took Bathsheeba as his wife. David was stricken by the realization of his sin when he was confronted by the prophet Nathan. David repented before God as the consequences of his transgression began to unfold, first in the death of Bathsheeba's son, and later in the rebellion of his oldest son, Absalom, who claimed the kingdom for his own. Yet King David refused to go into battle against his son, and even abandoned the throne in an act of penance, submissive to the will of God in his life. Absalom was subsequently killed by David's men, and David grieved at the loss of his son (II Samuel 11 through 19). David made serious mistakes in his life, with far-ranging effects on his family and his people. Yet he never placed the blame on anyone but himself, and bore the consequences of his own actions, recognizing his own sin. But the psalmist, Asaph, wrote, "David shepherded them with integrity of heart, with skillful hands he led them" (Psalm 78:72). Integrity is more than doing the right thing; integrity includes recognizing the truth and the conviction of the Holy Spirit, and admitting one's sin before God.

David is one of the best examples of the Godly warrior. But as we have seen in our Bible review, David was not the only warrior of his day. His best friend, Jonathan, had the heart of a warrior also. In First Samuel 14, Jonathan, alone with his armor bearer, fearlessly attacked a Philistine outpost; God moved in his behalf and the Philistines were routed. First Samuel 22:1-2 tells about the variety of men who "gathered around" David when he was in exile under Saul's rule, and he became their leader. After David became king, he was surrounded by a large number of warriors who served him under their own free will, including Abner, who was probably one of the valiant men whose heart God touched under the service of King Saul. First Chronicles 11 and 12 list in detail the mighty men of God, warriors in David's kingdom, "fighting men who volunteered to serve in the ranks." One cannot doubt that these men were trained in combat; nor can one doubt that they were devoted to their master.

We know David was a master of the sling, and with his faith in God, he slew the giant and went on to lead Israel into peace with its enemies. As a young man, David understood that a warrior is a servant to the master and eventually became a master in his own right. It follows that the attributes of a warrior must always be subject to the master. It is important, then, to understand the concept of a master, to further understand the heart of a warrior, and better understand the heart of God.

King David mourns for Abner

The Concept of a Master

After consideration of David and the mighty men under his command, it is appropriate here to briefly consider the concept of a master. From a biblical perspective, God is the master over all and is deserving of the title. But in John 13, Jesus Christ set the example of a servant, and washed His disciples' feet. Then He said to them, "You call Me the Teacher (Master) and the Lord, and you are right in doing so, for that is what I am. If I then, your Lord and Teacher (Master) have washed your feet, you ought...to wash one another's feet [sic]" (John 13:13-14, Amplified Bible). Here Jesus shows the example of the master as teacher, in service to his students. James 3:1 states that a teacher is held to a higher standard, and so the Christian warrior master must take his training seriously, in order to show respect to his students, his peers, and his own teachers.

But Jesus is more than a teacher. Commonly known as the "Living Word," the Disciple John described Jesus like this:

> In the beginning was the Word, and the Word was with God, and the Word was God....The Word became flesh and made his dwelling among us. (John 1:1-14)

The Apostle Paul wrote to the people of Phillipi about Christ Jesus:

> Who being in very nature God, did not consider equality with God something to be grasped, but made himself nothing, taking the very nature of a servant. (Phillipians 2:6-7)

As God, Jesus is indeed the master of the universe, in the sense that He is in complete control over everything in His hand. And so the Christian warrior, as a mere human, seeks to master the only thing that he has any real control over, which is his own body, and that which he can hold in his hand.

The objective of the master warrior is to always be in complete control of the full suite of faculties and resources that are at his disposal, under any circumstances. Those faculties include emotions such as anger and fear, and all of the physiological senses of the body, including sight, hearing, skin perception (feeling or touch), smell, and taste, as well as that which is often referred to as a sixth sense or gut feeling, and in the case of a Christian, discernment. The resources available to the warrior include various parts of the body such as fingers, hands, elbows, feet, knees, head, and voice, as well as external implements that may range from non-apparent weapons such as a cane or the "jawbone of an ass," to more advanced weapons ranging from knives and swords to the modern technology of firearms and even fighter jets. The circumstances under which a warrior may be required to use his faculties and resources may range from full health, conditioning, and dexterity to impaired states caused by injury, pain, intoxication (poisoning), or duress. The master Christian warrior must train to be able to effectively control his actions and behavior under any combination of access or limitations to these attributes, to achieve his objectives.

In a third sense, the Bible is full of stories of masters who seem to have control over both servants and slaves, the difference being the servant is a servant as a result of his own choice, but the slave may be pressed into service against his will (similar to the difference between a warrior and a soldier, as described earlier). In Second Peter 2:19, the Disciple Peter writes, "For a man is a slave to whatever has mastered him." And Paul writes in First Corinthians 6:12, "Everything is permissible for me—but not everything is beneficial. Everything is permissible for me—but I will not be mastered by anything." But God told Cain in Genesis 4:1, "If you do what is right, will you not be accepted? But if you do not do what is right, sin is crouching at your door; it desires to have you, but you must master it." Cain failed to understand God's warning, and he murdered his own brother. The Christian warrior understands that sin is the ultimate enemy, because sin is a master that seeks to enslave. Therefore he strives to be a servant instead of a slave, because he understands the value of freedom, and he recognizes his true Master. The Christian warrior knows this truth: "For sin shall not be your master, because you are not under law, but under grace" (Romans 6:14). Therefore, the master Christian warrior freely chooses to serve God rather than be a slave to sin.

The perspective of the Bible held by a master Christian warrior provides an answer to the history of slavery contained therein. The reality of slavery in the world has a spiritual parallel in the history of mankind. God's desire to see His chosen people released from the oppression of the Egyptians is the same desire He had to see His people released from the oppression of the Philistines, which is the same desire He had to see the abolition of slavery in 19th century America, which is the same desire He has to see young women rescued from sexual slavery in India and other parts of the world today. Hebrews 13:8 says, "Jesus Christ is the same yesterday and today and forever." God "does not change like shifting shadows" (James 1:17). God's desire is also to see men and women rescued from the slavery of sin. Therefore, Christ necessarily died on the cross at Calvary to provide that opportunity.

Clearly, God designed mankind with a passion for freedom, and so He gave each person a free will. Perhaps it lives undiscovered, deep in the heart of some, but the passion for freedom permeates the heart of the Christian warrior. However, motivated by love, the Christian warrior must submit to God's authority to prevent oppressing those under his own authority. The Christian warrior must seek to master that which he can control with his hand, but never use his hand to oppress those under his tutelage, authority, or care. For these he must be the master teacher, leader, and protector, and must set an example for his charges to follow as Christ did, as a willing servant. And those charges must never question the authority of their own master or teacher, just as David never questioned the authority of King Saul. Herein is the paradox of the "servant-leader". The Christian warrior understands it, and he holds no resentment for the master that he freely serves, because the master is a servant also. There is mutual respect among proven warriors, just as David respected Abner, the general of King Saul's army who eventually submitted to King David's God-ordained authority. This mutual respect leads to the unity required to win battles and wars.

With his God-given love of freedom, the Christian warrior master teaches his students that certain things are worth fighting for. The Christian warrior must depend on the grace of God to overcome the control of his own sin, and he is moved by his understanding to fight when it is necessary, spiritually or physically. And with the spirit of God leading him and the power of God working through him, "the least [is] a match for a hundred and the greatest for a thousand" (I Chronicles 12:14), and so he fights to save himself and God's people from the oppression of the world and of sin. The Bible says this about the odds of winning:

> If you follow my decrees and are careful to obey my commands, I will send you rain in its season, and the ground will yield its crops and the trees of the field their fruit…I will grant peace in the land, and you will lie down and no one will make you afraid. I will remove savage beasts from the land, and the sword will not pass through your country.

You will pursue your enemies, and they will fall by the sword before you. Five of you will chase a hundred and a hundred of you will chase ten thousand, and your enemies will fall by the sword before you. (Leviticus 26:3-8)

"My children...love one another" (John 13:33-34). This is the motivation of the Christian martial arts master and warrior. It is the greatest expression of love to lay down one's life for another, and it is the next greatest expression of love to give one's life in service.

The Concept of a Master

David in prayer to God

The Warrior's Refreshment

One primary purpose of Christian martial arts is to train persons for spiritual battle. The Christian warrior is victorious by faith in Jesus Christ. This faith is the only way to win spiritual fights. These battles are not won by the power of mantra, human will, or creative thought.[1] Faith in Jesus Christ is the strategy for spiritual victory.

A key objective of a warrior is to know his enemy. If a warrior can understand the nature and intent of the enemy, the warrior can devise a plan to counter the tactics of his opponent. Regardless of the desire for peace, a fight may still be required, and depending on a number of factors, an effective defense can be maintained. However, the duration of the fight will depend on the strength and skill of the combatants. It is imperative that the wise warrior never underestimates the strength and will of his adversary. Fatigue and exhaustion can lead directly to injury, defeat, and death. To loosely paraphrase the American General George S. Patton from World War II, a dead warrior is a useless warrior and the object is to make the opponent the one who dies for his cause.

After Samson slew the thousand Philistines with his equine weapon, he was tired and thirsty. He cried out to God, and God provided a spring of fresh water to slake his thirst. Joshua marched around Jericho for six days before raising his battle cry. David inquired of the LORD before pursuing the raiders of Keilah. The appeal to God is vital for the Christian warrior to prevail.

After Joshua defeated Jericho with trumpets, he reconnoitered the land of Ai. The spies returned and gave Joshua this report, "Not all the people will have to go up against Ai. Send two or three thousand men to take it, and do not weary the people, for only a few men are there" (Joshua 7:3). Joshua listened to his agents and sent the lone battalion into war. But the men of Ai defeated them and thirty-six were killed. They fled from the rout and the "hearts of the people melted and became like water". Joshua ripped his shirt and fell before the LORD in prayer. As it turns out, when they plundered Jericho, Achan, son of Zerah, coveted the treasures and hid some in his tent. God revealed the sin of Achan that cost Israel the battle. Achan was put to death and Joshua went on to defeat the king of Ai.

In retrospect, the sin of pride of the Israelite spies is obvious. They assumed the Israelite army was superior and could easily defeat the men of Ai. Joshua and his men went into battle ill-prepared, took the victory for granted, and tasted bitter defeat. In contrast, consider Moses and the battle against the Amelekites, for which the outcome of the battle was uncertain. When Moses could no longer hold up his hands, Aaron and Hur stood beside him, and together they prevailed (Exodus 17:8-13). Many times people overestimate their ability, fail to plan appropriately, and refuse to accept help because of their pride. Haughtiness, arrogance, and conceit are diseases of the warrior's heart.

The Disciple Peter told us that our enemy the devil "prowls around like a roaring lion, looking for someone to devour" (I Peter 5:8). The Disciple John told us that the "thief wants to kill, rob and destroy" (John 10:10). Our enemy is intent on destruction, but his strategy in battle is not direct. Discouragement, distraction, and division are weapons of a smart opponent.[2] But pride is the most subtle weapon of the evil one, for with it he causes our side to lose effectiveness. He even gains troops on his side of the battle, when men and women refuse to come to Christ because of their foolish pride. King David poignantly remarked, "The fool says in his heart 'There is no God'" (Psalm 14:1). The Bible says, "God opposes the proud but gives grace to the humble" (Proverbs 3:34, I Peter 5:5). With pride before God, the Christian warrior finds that his battle is no longer the same because he subverts his own Commander—the true, Ultimate Warrior. Because God is indomitable, His adversaries will not prevail.

The proper response to the attack of our spiritual enemy is humble prayer and intercession.[3] The popular Christian evangelist from Germany, Reinhard Bonnke, said, "Prayer opens up a vast arsenal of superior weapons...when we move in the spirit, we will always find the Achilles heel of the evil one...the fundamental nature of Christianity is the art of the impossible...the guard at the door of the heart is humility."[4]

In the Christian fiction novel, "This Present Darkness," author Frank Peretti paints a chilling picture of the demonic forces at spiritual warfare in the world around us, even in the same room in which we sit. But he also paints a vivid picture of the guardian angels, either beaten down by the demons or rejuvenated by the prayers of the saints to beat the demons back. This fantastic story is closer to the truth than the popular angel worship that we see in the world today. But the Bible is clear that we have guardian angels. The Psalmist sings:

> If you make the most high your dwelling
> Even the LORD, who is my refuge
> Then no harm will befall you,
> No disaster will come near your tent.
> For he will command his angels concerning you
> To guard you in all your ways;
> They will lift you up in their hands,
> So that you will not strike your foot against a stone.
> You will tread upon the lion and the cobra;
> You will trample the great lion and the serpent.
> "Because he loves me," says the LORD,
> "I will rescue him; I will protect him,
> For he acknowledges my name.
> He will call upon me, and I will answer him;
> I will be with him in trouble,
> I will deliver him and honor him.
> With long life will I satisfy him
> And show him my salvation. (Psalm 91:9-16)

It is important to note that it is God who commands the angels, not man. It is the man who calls out to God. But the attitude of the heart must be checked. One cannot call on

God in his pride and expect God to answer. It is only in repentance that the heart of man can be transformed.

Repentance is the cup for the Christian warrior's refreshment. Prayer is the vessel through which the cleansing blood of Jesus Christ flows into the warrior's heart. The blood of Jesus is the basis for the forgiveness of sins, and the only basis in which a person can enter the presence of God, without His righteous judgment. Here the Christian warrior can intercede with God, and He moves on the warrior's behalf, according to His wisdom. In repentance and prayer, the "living water" of Jesus Christ (John 4:10) refreshes the Christian warrior. The master warrior King David sets the example:

> Have mercy on me, O God,
> According to your unfailing love;
> According to your great compassion
> Blot out my transgressions
> Wash away all my iniquity
> And cleanse me from my sin.
> For I know my transgressions,
> And my sin is always before me.
> Against you, you only, have I sinned
> And done what is evil in your sight,
> So that you are proved right when you speak
> And justified when you judge…
> Wash me, and I will be whiter than snow…
> Create in me a pure heart, O God,
> And renew a steadfast spirit within me.
> Do not cast me from your presence

Or take your Holy Spirit from me.
Restore to me the joy of your salvation
And grant me a willing spirit, to sustain me.
Then I will teach transgressors your ways,
And sinners will turn back to you.
Save me from bloodguilt, O God,
The God who saves me,
And my tongue will sing of your righteousness.
O Lord, Open my lips,
And my mouth will declare your praise.
You do not delight in sacrifice, or I would bring it;
You do not take pleasure in burnt offerings.
The sacrifices of God are a broken spirit;
A broken and contrite heart, O God,
You will not despise. (Psalm 51:1-17)

The Warrior's Refreshment

The beginning of violence

The Need

Men and women with heavy suits stand by day and night to battle fires. Sirens wail as paramedics race to stop the bleeding veins. Doctor's steady hands perform intricate surgery inside the womb. Police detectives sift for clues to solve heinous crimes. Courts deliberate to convict the murderer. Society places an untold value on life because of the voice of God.

When Adam and Eve stumbled out of the garden, time was set in motion and mankind as we know it began. It was not long before the first teenager copped an attitude. Unchecked, Cain murdered his brother Abel, sassed God, and violence spread across the land. God was grieved and in pain from the wickedness of men, so he sent the waters to cleanse the world and start over (Genesis 4 through 6). Clearly moved by the devastation, God made a covenant never to flood the earth again, and he said to Noah, "For your lifeblood I will surely demand an accounting…from each man, too, I will demand an accounting for the life of his fellow man. Whoever sheds the blood of man, by man shall his blood be shed; for in the image of God has God made man" (Genesis 9:5-6). Cain was wrong; I am my brother's keeper.

Over the millennia, the nature of man has not really changed. But a man changes with time, just as a child grows up. Teenagers are not the cause of society's ills. Young men and women are the cells of life that the disease of the world attacks. Their fallow minds are fertile ground on which the world and the Church sow their seeds. The weeds are tall.

On April 20, 1999, two troubled teens waged an armed assault on their school and slaughtered twelve innocent and helpless classmates and a teacher. Their violence made Columbine High School in Littleton, Colorado, known in every home in America. Those were not the first school shooters, but they were the most notorious, until the lone college student rampaged across the campus of Virginia Tech, killing 32 people, and shook the world all the way to Korea. Why anyone would idolize these killers is a mystery to most people. There is a fascination with violence in society that defies an easy explanation apart from the fallen nature of man. However, these spectacular events are rare outside of Hollywood. But gruesome murders, robbery, rape, and other brutal crimes happen every day, around the world.

The youth of the 21st century are being ripped apart by the current of ideas that wash the landscape like an ocean, and the battle for their minds is as fierce as the violence that covered the earth before Noah's flood. The teenagers drown outside the Church, with wires in their ears gushing torrents of gibberish that only they can decode. They rebel in a perfectly natural fashion of darkness and gloom, draped over their bodies like a trench coat of death. Weapons of destruction are hidden on video games and in diaries in their rooms. Explosions of suicide haunt their sleep.

Boys smack each other down with folding chairs in vacant lots behind neighborhoods of families with children adrift in the vanity of the stars. A lonely girl paints her face in an empty mirror, with no regard for the beauty in her heart or the industry of her hands. The children's monitor is a flat screen and their discipline is a television schedule. Like hydroponic plants in synthetic soil, the children grow in the lifelessness of a life apart from Jesus Christ.

But these kids are not stupid. Nor are they all caught up in the schemes of the world. Most of them are ordinary or outstanding young people simply trying to learn how to survive in an overwhelming world. All of them see through curtains of duplicity with x-ray vision. Their capacity for accomplishment is limited only by their training. They are the same flesh and blood for which God demands an accounting, each with the potential of their untapped talent. But unless they learn the proper context for fighting, they are sheep without sheepdogs in a pack of wolves. Unless the youth learn to fight and win spiritual battles, they will be devoured by the deception of the enemy of their souls.

As it is, the young people grow up being told by pop psychologists that it is wrong to fight, but they fight anyway. If the boys are not in the backyard wrestling, they are inside watching the actors do it on TV. The so-called "professional" wrestling entertainment market is geared for teenage boys and young men, and it has flourished over the last four decades in spite of its hokey script. It is no wonder that boys imitate it; fighting is what boys and men do. Or rather, it is what they are capable of, and what they are capable at. The popularity of hand-to-hand combat is reflected in the rise of sport fighting on television. Boxing fades as "no holds barred" cage fighting and international team fighting take the spotlight. Taekwondo recently joined classic Judo and ancient Greco Roman wrestling as an official Olympic sport.[1] Sport fighting, which has a long history, is not the problem. The problem is that the Masked Preacher and Mr. Death are the role models these kids see.

Young people need role models. Kids need leaders and they find them. But too often, those leaders are the neighborhood bullies or gang leaders who dominate the child and push him into a form of servitude. Intimidation is used to pressure young men into rights of passage, or else they cannot belong to the gang. Outside the gang, the kid is defenseless, and so he goes along out of self-preservation and fear, or he lies to himself and joins to be cool. Christian martial arts training offers teenagers an alternative through which they can find several characteristics that young men desire and which gangs exploit; for example, sense of membership, association, identity, fellowship, physical security, and comfort. Gangs, which have a long history, are not the problem. In America, the First Amendment to the Constitution guarantees the freedom of association—a freedom worth fighting for. The problem is the criminal leaders of the gangs whom King Solomon wrote about in the tenth century Before Christ:

> My son, if sinners entice you, do not give in to them.

If they say, "Come along with us;
Let's lie in wait for someone's blood,
Let's waylay some harmless soul;
Let's swallow them alive, like the grave,
And whole, like those who go down into the pit;
We will get all sorts of valuable plunder;
Throw in your lot with us,
And we will share a common purse."
My son, do not go along with them, do not set
foot on their paths;
For their feet rush into sin, they are swift to shed
blood.
How useless to spread a net in full view of the
birds!
These men lie in wait for their own blood;
They waylay only themselves!
Such is the end of all who go after ill-gotten gain;
It takes away the lives of those who get it.
(Proverbs 1:10-19)

All things said, the majority of young men and women grow up without getting in much, if any, trouble. Many are even respectful of their parents. Often they are referred to as straight, and most of them do well enough in school. They hear a trumpet blast and join a team, football or soccer, wrestling perhaps; maybe they even join a traditional martial arts class such as karate or taekwondo. Those who recognize the sound of the shofar often become fire fighters or crime fighters, or join the military. Some of those who enlist were on the edge, and more often than not, the discipline of the fighting culture brought them into a life of integrity and honor. Many young men and women make careers in the military, filling an actual or indirect warrior's role. Active and veteran service men and women make up a significant percentage of the Church. For these, the Church must embrace the concept of Christian martial arts training and combat; otherwise, if the Church believes that Christian martial art is an oxymoron, it must tell these brave men and women to leave, or give up their warrior's call. There is a battle between good and evil in the world, and it is not always a spiritual battle. Someone has to fight on the side of good in both the spiritual and the physical realms.

The youth in America and the world need to know that there is more to being a Christian than listening to a mealy-mouthed preacher feeding pabulum to a bunch of milk toast weaklings who do not have the courage to go outside in a March wind. Even Jesus was not timid, but answered the challenge of those who tried to kill him, and called them liars and children of the devil (John 8:12-59). The Church needs to understand that youth around the world are worth fighting for. However, only the young people can defend themselves; Adam could not protect Abel from Cain. How quickly we send them into the battle of their lives with no defense.

Sooner or later, our children will be required to fight for what they believe in, and maybe those other things that are important, such as standing up to a bully or a killer or a tyrant. They need Christian training on the immeasurable value of a soul and the great sacrifice that is required to save each one. They need Christian training on the terrible decision one must make in order to take another person's life. They need Christian training on the proper way to handle the awesome power God has given them in their minds and their hands and their feet. They need Christian training on the righteous defense of a brother or a sister or a nation.

The Law

The Authority to Fight

The risk of death in fighting raises the specter of lethality. For the warrior to defend effectively means that lethal force may ultimately be required. However, the justification for lethal force is an exceptionally tight standard, and as we have seen, God will hold a man accountable for the death of another man by his hands. Because of God's decree, murder is a crime ingrained in the laws of nations around the world. But not all killing is murder. In many jurisdictions, murder is judged according to the intent of the killer. For example, to kill intentionally with malice and forethought is generally considered "first degree" murder and is judged more severely than to kill accidentally, i.e., manslaughter. These laws are generally consistent with legal principles outlined in the Holy Scriptures. In Numbers 35, God ordered the Israelites to establish cities of refuge where the accidental killer could flee and be safe from revenge until a trial could establish his innocence or guilt. But even if found innocent of murder, which is to say he was guilty of manslaughter, he was banished to live there until the high priest died. This chapter of Scripture is also notable for its call for capital punishment. But in modern civilization, vengeance killing in retribution for murder is not tolerated, unless it is conducted by the state. Consider what the Apostle Paul wrote in Romans 13:1-4:

> Everyone must submit himself to the governing authorities, for there is no authority except that which God has established. The authorities that exist have been established by God. Consequently, he who rebels against the authority is rebelling against what God has instituted, and those who do so will bring judgment on themselves. For rulers hold no terror for those who do right, but for those who do wrong. Do you want to be free from fear of the one in authority? Then do what is right and he will commend you. For he is God's servant to do you good. But if you do wrong, be afraid, for he does not bear the sword for nothing. He is God's servant, an agent of wrath to bring punishment on the wrong doer [sic].

From a New Testament perspective, God has clearly relegated the matters of law enforcement and war to the "governing authorities," which is to say the state, regardless of its political nature. But He did not tell the Christians to quit or avoid being involved in these institutions. Rather, He calls for "soldiers" to act with justice and contentment (Luke 3:14). Jesus even stayed with Zacchaeus the tax collector, and proclaimed the salvation that came into his home (Luke 19:1-10). Paul went on to say:

> Therefore it is necessary to submit to the authorities, not only because of possible punishment, but because of conscience. This is why you pay taxes, for the authorities are God's servants, who give their full time to governing. (Romans 13:5-6)

If the authorities are God's servants, then the Church should be training people in biblical moral principles and sending them to serve in those positions of authority, whether they are political, regulatory, military, or law enforcement. In carrying out their official and lawful orders and duties, the judge and the executioner of the capital criminal, the police officer who must use lethal force in the line of duty, and the soldier or warrior who kills in the battles of war are not guilty of murder because they are lawfully authorized to fight or kill as necessary, on behalf of the state. This authority does not diminish the serious nature of spilling blood. Numbers 35:33 says, "Do not pollute the land where you are. Bloodshed pollutes the land, and atonement cannot be made for the land on which blood has been shed, except by the blood of the one who shed it." The great warrior King David, anointed and set apart by God, was not allowed to build a temple for the Ark of the Covenant, because he was "a warrior and [had] shed blood" (I Chronicles 28:3). But what of the man or woman who kills in self-defense or defense of others?

When Jesus Christ told his disciples to get a sword in Luke 22:36, He was foreshadowing the suffering that was to come, both for himself and for the Church.[1] Referring to himself, Jesus quoted Isaiah 53:12, "And he was numbered with the transgressors." The persecution of the believer was prophesied by Jesus in Luke 21:12:

> But before all this [strife], they will lay hands on you and persecute you. They will deliver you to synagogues and prisons, and you will be brought before kings and governors, and all on account of my name.

And so it is necessary to distinguish the basis for self-defense. Is the defense against persecution for one's religious convictions? Or is it against random criminal violence and bodily harm? Or is it against assault from someone close; for example, domestic violence? Or is it an attack on a lawfully assembled group of people? Regarding persecution, Jesus went on to say in Luke 21:13-15:

> This [presence before kings and governors] will result in your being witnesses to them. But make up your mind not to worry beforehand how you will defend yourselves. For I will give you the words and wisdom that none of your adversaries will be able to resist or contradict.

But regarding the defense against bodily harm, we must return to Paul's references to the authority of the law and to the Book of Isaiah. Isaiah 53 contains prophecies about the Christ, and Isaiah 54 contains prophecies about the Church. Consider Isaiah 54:12-17:

I will make your battlements of rubies, your gates of sparkling jewels, and all your walls of precious stones. All your sons will be taught by the LORD, and great will be your children's peace. In righteousness you will be established: Tyranny will be far from you; you will have nothing to fear. Terror will be far removed; it will not come near you. If anyone does attack you, it will not be my doing; whoever attacks you will surrender to you. See, it is I who created the blacksmith who fans the coals into flame and forges a weapon fit for its work. And it is I who have created the destroyer to work havoc; no weapon formed against you will prevail, and you will refute every tongue that accuses you.

It is interesting to note that references to self-defense are often coupled with references to persecution. When we follow God's laws, he not only blesses us, but our enemies who attack us, physically or spiritually, will be defeated and refuted before us (Deuteronomy 28:1-7).

Under the authority of the law, including most written codes and the "law of the land" for eons, the right to defend against bodily harm is paramount, whether the objective of preventing such harm is personal self-defense, defense of others, or group defense. The argument that Jesus would expect a person or assembly to simply yield at the risk of injury or death if attacked, or to avert their eyes and refuse to help when someone else is attacked, is absurd. Although the Christian should never desire to be responsible for the death of another, the authority of the law often gives him absolution for lethal force under certain cases of self-defense or defense of others. The reference to a "well regulated militia" in the Second Amendment to the Constitution of the United States of America is a decree for the lawful assembly and preparation for group defense, above and beyond the defense of the individual.

Some jurisdictions even grant the right to use lethal force in defense of property. However, Jesus taught about a higher road to follow:

> Love your enemies, do good to those who hate you, bless those who curse you, pray for those who mistreat you. If someone strikes you on the cheek, turn to him the other also. If someone takes your cloak, do not stop him from taking your tunic…Do to others as you would have them do to you. (Luke 6:27-31)

These are rules for daily living. Jesus was clearly teaching us to be kind and humble, and not to be vindictive. When Jesus taught the people to turn the other cheek, he was telling them to avoid retaliation when insulted. He was not teaching them to be weak and roll over on their back like a submissive dog. The sword that he subsequently told the disciples to get was a type of dagger used by the Jews for self-defense, and he was telling them to be prepared for the difficult times that lay ahead for the Church.[2] Jesus' orders before His arrest authorized the Church to provide for and defend itself (Luke 22:36) with the same authority

He had previously sent the Disciples to drive out demons, heal the sick, and preach the Gospel (Luke 9:1-6). The extent to which the Church should prepare can be seen in three case histories of "church defense" that occurred within the current decade.

In 2003, a pastor of a small independent church in Alaska installed a baby monitor to serve as a burglar alarm in response to a rash of burglaries in the area. The monitor served its purpose one evening when two men broke into the church. The pastor left his adjacent home and entered the building armed with a large-caliber handgun. The men were in the basement kitchen when they realized they had been discovered. The intruders fled up the stairs on which the pastor was descending, passing him in close quarters in the dark stair well. The pastor shot both men in the back as they fled the church. One man died in the yard, and the other died soon after his escape. The court eventually acquitted the pastor of manslaughter. He stated to investigators that he was "scared to death."[3] Although the law justified him, it appears that he failed Jesus' command to give up his tunic to the man who would steal his cloak. The independent pastor apparently did not have a professional security plan, and he violated the most basic security protocol when he entered alone into a dark building in which he knew there were intruders. In review, it is too easy to be critical from the comfort of distance. The value of training to be prepared to use the level of force necessary for the seriousness of the situation cannot be overemphasized.

In stark contrast, in 2007, a disgruntled young man acted on his animosity toward the Church and knocked on the door of a missionary training center in Colorado. With cold blood he shot and killed the young man and woman who answered. Presciently, across town, one of the largest churches in America increased the level of its security team on duty the next Sunday morning, after hearing news of the event. This church had previously authorized a formal security plan that included trained personnel from the church membership who <u>volunteered</u> for the role.[4] The murderous young man arrived on the church campus and threw smoke grenades at an entrance. He then drove to another entrance and, in the parking lot, murdered two girls and wounded their father. The murderer then entered the building armed with a paramilitary style, semi-automatic rifle, at least two handguns, and a substantial amount of ammunition. But inside the door was a trained and authorized Christian warrior. Armed only with a handgun, the woman emerged from cover and confronted the shooter. She testified, "God made me strong," as she engaged the killer with steady hands in a gunfight that left the man on the floor and her unscathed.[5] In a twist of irony of biblical proportions, the coroner determined that the man died from a self-inflicted gunshot.[6] The conscience of the heroine, Jeanne Assam, was cleared of the fate of the man's soul.

In 2008, the unpopular results of a political election led to widespread rioting in Kenya. Gangs from a disaffected ethnic group began to hack and murder people from the victorious politician's ethnic group. Accusations of voting irregularities were followed by accusations of political motivation for the ensuing mayhem. In one grim incident, the rioters assaulted a church where a number of people had sought refuge. At this church, with only "boys who were guarding it," 50 innocent people, including women and children, were literally incinerated by politically and ethnically enflamed fire.[7] Although somewhat unusual, the situation in Kenya is not the first example of the murderous disrespect toward the Church in the world today. A building does not make a sanctuary. The Spirit of God—and the people on guard—make a refuge safe.

The Church is given the authority from God, and must accept the responsibility, to prepare for such contingencies as described above, whether in the church building or in society at large. The Apostle Paul told the saints in Ephesus to "be strong in the Lord and in his mighty power" (Ephesians 6:10), to put on God's armor, and to "stand your ground, and <u>after you have done everything</u> [emphasis added], to stand" (Ephesians 6:13).

To turn the cheek on insult is a Christian thing to do; to stop a murderer or a murderous mob from killing is a thing that Christian warrior's do. Defense of the weak and the innocent is an act of righteousness. Such actions were exemplified by Abram when he rescued Lot and King David when he rescued the people of Keilah. For a man to strike a woman, or a child, or a weakling, or to strike in response to insult or irrational fear is an act of cowardice. There are times when a person must stand up for one's dignity and fight back in some capacity, as in the case of assault, attempted rape, an abused wife, or a bullied child. In all these things, it is imperative to use discernment regarding the nature of the threat and its motivation. Personal self-defense is the area in which the Christian must be most careful. In personal self-defense, the Christian warrior must exemplify the characteristics of the warrior God that benefit us all on a daily basis:

> But you, O Lord, are a compassionate and gracious God, slow to anger, abounding in love and faithfulness. (Psalm 86:15)
> (Exodus 34:6, Numbers 14:18, Nehemiah 9:17, Psalm 103:8, and Jonah 4:2 are all similar.)

As the Disciple James wrote, "Everyone should be quick to listen, slow to speak and slow to become angry, for man's anger does not bring about the righteous life that God desires" (James 1:20). Because God is "longsuffering" is the reason why Christians do not riot when God is insulted, even in the face of blasphemy. But they are willing to fight when necessary.

Just as there are various degrees of murder, there are various levels of honor in fighting and dying. To die in the valor of combat for a righteous cause is not the same as suicide in a murderous explosion of innocent lives. To die a martyr as a result of persecution is not the same as to die from an act of criminal violence. Paul admonished Titus to remind the people to be obedient to the authorities and to "be no brawlers" (Titus 3:2 KJV), which is to say, be a man (or woman) of peace, and not be contentious to the point of fighting. Assault and battery, street fighting, and underground fight clubs are against the law. God desires for us to turn to doing good because of His great mercy and to turn away from malice, hatefulness, quarreling, and anger (Titus 3:3-8).

The motivation of a Christian warrior to fight must be love, whether it is in self-defense, defense of others, or group defense. The Apostle Paul provided clarity about the proper attitude that we should have toward our fellow man and his institutions:

> Give everyone what you owe him: If you owe taxes, pay taxes; if revenue, then revenue; if respect, then respect, if honor, then honor. Let no debt remain outstanding, except the continuing debt to love one another, for he who loves his fellowman has fulfilled the law. The commandments, "Do not commit adultery," "Do not murder," "Do not steal," "Do not covet," and whatever other commandment there may be, are summed up in this one rule: "Love your neighbor as yourself." Love does no harm to its neighbor. Therefore love is the fulfillment of the law. (Romans 13: 8-10)

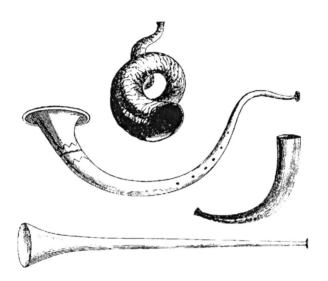

Shofars and trumpets

One Long Blast

When young David fled from murderous King Saul to Nob, he asked Ahimelech the priest if he had any weapons. Imagine David's surprise when Ahimelech produced Goliath's sword, hidden in the temple. David said, "There is none like it; give it to me" (I Samuel 21:1-9). When Samson was on his way to Philistia, he killed a lion with his bare hands, and later killed a thousand Philistine's with a donkey's jawbone. Shamgar, son of Anath, saved Israel with an oxgoad. Faithful Joshua used a ram's horn to bring down the walls of Jericho. The weapon doesn't control a man; a man controls the weapon. It is the attitude of the heart that determines how the weapon is controlled. When John the Baptist, the cousin of Jesus Christ, preached his call to repentance, the soldier asked what he should do. The Baptist did not tell the soldier to lay down his weapons, but said, "Don't extort money, and don't accuse people falsely—be content with your pay" (Luke 3:14). Jesus healed the paralyzed servant of the Centurion after he marveled at the extent of the man's faith and his understanding of authority (Matthew 8:8-10). Training the attitude of the heart is fundamental for Christian martial arts.

It is important to note that not all fighting is intended to be lethal, and not all fighting is conducted in anger. No one expects to see high school wrestlers fight to the death.

Indeed the high school wrestling team is authorized to fight within the bounds of the law, and the rules of the match. They even fight inside the school and the fair winner is exalted. If a punch is thrown, accidentally or on purpose, a penalty or disqualification will occur. But if those guys take it outside and go to the ground, they risk suspension and even arrest by local law enforcement.

Within the context of the hundreds of sports sanctioning groups around the world, fighting is legal, generally speaking. Sanctioned competitive fighting has occurred for thousands of years and includes Greco-Roman wrestling, boxing, and pankration (pan-cra-tee-on) in the ancient Olympics.[1] Pankration, similar to the currently popular "mixed martial arts," was reportedly appropriated by the Romans into the "blood sports" of the gladiators, and was subsequently banned by the Christian Byzantine Emperor Theodosius I in 393 A. D.[2] Currently, a range of sanctioned combat sports are available with various degrees of credibility. For example, within wrestling, the pseudo-sport of professional wrestling does not carry the same prestige as that of the genuine Olympic sport of freestyle wrestling. In the eastern style martial arts, there is a huge range of credibility, or lack thereof, even outside of Hollywood, because of the unbelievable claims of the power of the martial arts, as well as the proliferation of braggarts and their institutions.[3] Such boasting is not new in the martial arts world. King David executed the Amalekite who falsely claimed to have killed the critically wounded, King Saul. David proclaimed, "Your blood be on your own head. Your own mouth testified against you when you said, 'I killed the LORD's anointed'" (II Samuel 1:1-16). The point is that under the authority of the sanctioning body and its rules, there is no apparent prohibition in the Scriptures from participation in combat, and by extension, combat sports. In fact, the observant Apostle Paul said:

> Though I am free and belong to no man, I make myself a slave to everyone, to win as many as possible...To those under the law, I became like one under the law...I have become all things to all men so that by all possible means I might save some. I do all this for the sake of the gospel, that I may share in its blessings...Run in such a way as to get the prize. Everyone who competes in the games goes into strict training. They do it to get a crown that will not last; but we do it to get a crown that will last forever. Therefore I do not run like a man running aimlessly; I do not fight like a man beating the air. No, I beat my body and make it my slave so that after I have preached to others, I myself will not be disqualified for the prize. (I Corinthians 9:19-27)

Like the Christian warrior in a real-life situation, the Christian "warrior-in-training" who desires to be involved in combat sports must examine his motivation and use discernment when picking an organization within which to participate. To be sure, not all are honorable, or worthy of membership. But there are honorable men and women and their associations within the broadly defined, martial arts community. The Church will benefit by recognizing and sanctioning the warriors-in-training within its congregations.

To establish a successful Christian martial arts training program, the instructor is the key. He must be a man of faith in Jesus Christ with an intimate understanding of the Holy Scriptures. The instructor must be sensitive to the spirit of discernment. He must have a clue of the awesome power of the Holy Spirit. He must be a man of prayer and worship and humble spirit. The Christian Research Institute, a respected watchdog of church theology and cult research, conducted a detailed review of the rising popularity of martial arts and its incursion into the Church. In their two-part essay, "Enter the Dragon? Wrestling With The Martial Arts Phenomenon," the researchers examined the nature of traditional, Eastern martial arts from a biblical perspective. Because many of the religious components cannot be reconciled with sound Christian doctrine, the conclusion was that the instructor must be qualified to discern and teach Christian truth.[4]

Much like the Old Testament fighters and their battles, with their various weapons, the nature or form of the fighting is not the issue. The important thing to note is that the physical training of warriors is nowhere near as important as the spiritual curriculum. The physical training is simply the medium through which the training of the heart and mind is delivered. Any Olympic-sanctioned sport such as wrestling or taekwondo is sufficiently devoid of religious overtones to be suitable for adaptation as a Christian martial art. Respectable sanctioning groups already exist. In-school archery programs, riflery, and fencing are martial sports that could be used to teach boys and girls, men and women, about the attributes of a Christian warrior. Curriculums can be developed for physical education classes in Christian schools or colleges. Churches can develop effective family-based ministries through Christian martial arts training programs. Because most churches already provide some level of security for their parishioners and priests, providing elementary training is not a giant leap. Christian professional security services and militia represent an advanced or mature level of Christian martial arts training and are becoming more imperative around the world where lawlessness prevails. As mentioned, the Church must provide the fundamental teaching for the people who serve in authority outside the Church, where church members have access to serve in those positions.

Finding qualified instructors is not the challenge. Men and women will rise to the opportunity given them by the Church to fulfill God's calling in their lives.[5] But the warriors and the singers and the priests march in separate columns. Veterans, high school coaches, hunters, law enforcement officers, and others are qualified to teach boxing, wrestling, archery, small-arms shooting, and other martial disciplines. Black belts in church clothes pepper congregations across the globe, waiting on church leadership to affirm what they already know. Many of these warrior teachers languish in the choir, separated from God's purpose in their lives.

The Church simply needs to provide the following:

1. A blessing on the program.
2. Space, preferably the size of a small gym, two or three nights per week.
3. One long blast on the shofar.

Then watch God's people grow.

WARNING: BE ON GUARD FOR ENEMY ATTACK. Unlike Goliath, the Christian's adversary is not content to wait at the front lines and bellow out his challenges. He has no compulsions against attacking the school and will target both the leadership and the students. Attacks will come from all directions, including from within the ranks. The minions of Screwtape[6] will double their efforts to infiltrate the Church and influence the believers with their back-biting strategies, including slander and ridicule. Prayer defenses, perseverance, and integrity must be maintained, in addition to protecting the physical perimeter.

One Long Blast

Trained archers

A Model for Discipleship

Many forms of traditional martial arts have long histories of Eastern religious influence. Taekwondo, a relatively young expression of the influence of martial arts on Korea,[1] is examined in the next three chapters. The World Taekwondo Headquarters, known as the Kukkiwon, in Seoul, Korea, describes the cultural and religious influences over thousands of years leading up to the development of taekwondo.[2]

Even though taekwondo is currently promoted as an Olympic sport, some Grand Masters still contend that the tenants of taekwondo lead to "enlightenment or some sort of mystic consciousness or divine union."[3] These attributes and their history make many Christians uncomfortable and often opposed to martial arts training. However, much of taekwondo is quite compatible with Christianity. For example, taekwondo philosophy includes "love and benevolence, magnanimity, sympathy and character", as well as the five tenets of taekwondo: courtesy, integrity, perseverance, self-control, and indomitable spirit.[4] In comparison, the "fruits" of the Christian spirit include: "love, joy, peace, patience, kindness, goodness, faithfulness, gentleness and self-control. Against such things there is no law" (Galatians 5:22-23).

Because we have this specific assurance from the Holy Bible, Christian Taekwondo is a suitable and effective curriculum to model discipleship and promote Christian philosophy. The Apostle Paul said that physical training is of some value, but spiritual training is of great value (I Timothy 4:8). The beginning student of taekwondo quickly learns that one does not begin with complete understanding. The white belt must be trained in the art in order to advance through the ranks of the colored belts. In Christian Taekwondo, this advancement should be coupled with specific learning objectives to actively promote the most important part of the student's development, which is spiritual growth. For example, spiritual training can be accomplished by requiring the student to memorize a specific scripture associated with each belt rank in order to advance. At one church-based Christian Taekwondo club, the white belt must memorize the club motto: "I can do all things through Christ which strengtheneth me" (Philippians 4:13 KJV).

To promote additional spiritual training, scriptures about essential Christian doctrine or the Roman Road could be required for yellow, orange, green, and the subsequent colored belts used to denote rank and accomplishment. By combining these teaching devices with regular devotionals, prayer, and fellowship, the masters of Christian Taekwondo and church leadership can rest assured that God's word will not return empty (Isaiah 55:11).

As the student grows in learning both the martial art of taekwondo and Christian philosophy, improvement and additional actions are expected. For example, a red belt is required to lead testing and properly demonstrate specific techniques that the testee must perform. In fact, upper-ranked students are expected not only to show significant improvement in taekwondo techniques, but also to set examples for the lower-ranked students at every class and tournament. Although leadership and reaching out to lower-ranked belts is taught to all belt levels, the red belts, junior black belts, and first dan (degree) black belts must show noticeable improvements in this area. In Christian Taekwondo, these advanced belts are expected to exemplify Christian qualities, and help the lower-ranked students with their spiritual growth as well. The will to help other students improve in both their physical and spiritual training is an expression of love. As students learn to love one another by helping one another, then they know that they are becoming Disciples of Christ. Jesus said "By this all men will know that you are my disciples, if you love one another" (John 13:35).

Sooner or later in any martial art, the student will be faced with the religious aspects of the particular discipline, whether it is taekwondo, karate, or kung fu, among many others. In Christian Taekwondo, spiritual exposure is elementary, in accordance with the words of Jesus Christ, who said, "Let the little children come to me and do not hinder them, for the kingdom of heaven belongs to such as these"(Matthew 19:14). In other words, the white belts are introduced to Christian teaching from the beginning, and Christian principles are taught to all belts in every class. At the second dan, the taekwondo student is fully qualified to be the teacher and open a dojang (studio) as the sole instructor. Therefore, the second dan black belt must realize and accept this additional responsibility, because as the Disciple James said, "...you know that we who teach will be judged more strictly" (James 3:1). In Christian Taekwondo, the second dan black belt must embrace the words of Jesus Christ to the spiritually mature, "...go and make disciples of all nations...teaching them to obey everything I have commanded you..." (Matthew 28:19-20). This responsibility requires a commitment to discipleship, which is indeed the calling of every Christian.

Simply because the black belt is expected to become a teacher does not mean that he or she is no longer a student. Even the advanced black belts and masters must continue to learn, or fail to understand the nature and limits of their own existence. As a tree matures, it continues to need a source of water and nourishment if it is to bear fruit season after season. The master of Christian Taekwondo realizes that this nourishment must come from "the river of the water of life...flowing from the throne of God..." (Revelation 22:1). The revelation of Jesus Christ, who is the source of that river, is the true enlightenment that will be found by those who seek the truth in their spiritual development. The beauty and paradox of Christianity is that the divine union, which results in the mystic consciousness known as the "joy of salvation," is not reserved for the esoteric, but is found as a white belt in one's spiritual development. Christian Taekwondo provides a setting to promote the wholesome values of Christianity while teaching the practical and physical benefits of the martial arts. Children learn respect and discipline, awkward teenagers learn balance and dexterity, and timid adults gain fitness and self-confidence. These are just a few of the physical benefits of taekwondo. As the student of Christian Taekwondo progresses through the belts, the significance of being a Disciple of Jesus Christ is realized. The spiritual benefits from becoming a Master Disciple through spiritual growth are immeasurable. This transformation will bring rewards both in this life and in the eternal life to come.

Bubishi grapplers

Reconciling

the

Kiap to Christ

The student of martial arts is taught from the very beginning that there are certain attributes one must develop that are much more important than physical training and discipline. These attributes are intended to help build one's self not only physically, but also emotionally and spiritually. The emotional and spiritual principles used in taekwondo are philosophical teachings that stress concepts such as honor, loyalty, courage, bravery, integrity, honesty, respect, morals, love, benevolence, magnanimity with humility, and compassion.

Another important attribute often mentioned but seldom emphasized is that the taekwondo student must be concerned about the pursuit of truth. Truth is the highest standard for which any student should aspire, for without it, all other tenets of emotional and spiritual training are in vain. To lay a solid foundation for training in taekwondo, one must possess an unyielding desire to know the truth about every aspect of his training. To understand the truth about the "kiap," an audible technique used in the martial arts, one must know the history of taekwondo, the truth about the universe, and how to reconcile the kiap to Christ.

Taekwondo is a modern expression of ancient traditional martial arts and kicking games whose history can be traced back 2,000 to 3,000 years to the ancient Korean and Japanese cultures.[1] The roots of taekwondo and most Eastern martial arts were heavily influenced by traditional Buddhist religious doctrine. This religious doctrine was founded in the sixth century before Christ by Siddhartha Gautama, also known as Gautama Buddha. Buddha was a man in search of the truth who, according to legend, merely picked a flower in silence, and so began a major ascetic world religion.[2]

A fundamental concept of Buddhism is the dualism of the cosmos; in other words, the concepts of good and evil, darkness and light, and other juxtaposed antonyms symbolized by the Tae Guek, commonly recognized as the yin and yang. The kiap is a derivation of the "ki" or "chi," which in Buddhist philosophy represents an energy or life force that permeates the universe. Students of traditional taekwondo and other martial arts are encouraged to tap into this force to obtain personal benefit, whether in breaking a board or gaining spiritual, emotional, and physical health.[3]

In fact, these concepts of dualism and universal life force are not unique to taekwondo or Buddhism, but are used in other religious philosophies such as Zen Buddhism (a cultic offshoot of traditional Buddhism), Hinduism, and the New Age or "Cosmic Humanist" movement.[4] As an example, the student of yoga, a form of physical and spiritual exercise heavily influenced by Hinduism, practices a breathing exercise to control the "prana," also known as the ki, the universal life force that resides in the "chakra," an energy center of the body. In traditional taekwondo or other Eastern martial arts, the student is taught that the chakra through which the kiap emanates is located at the middle portion of the abdomen or the solar plexus.

The yoga student is taught that the chakra is one of six spiritual energy centers in the body through which the Hindu serpent goddess Shakti rises from the base of the spine to unite with her consort Shiva, the seventh chakra, who resides in the forehead between the eyebrows. This union leads to the fulfillment of yoga, or union with Brahman, the Hindu concept of an unknowable and inexplicable god. The taekwondo student who uses the ki has simply failed to understand the ultimate purpose of this ancient religious concept.

To fully understand the truth about these philosophies, one must turn to the ancient writings of the Holy Scriptures, also known as the Holy Bible. By studying these writings, the seeker of truth learns that the universe is controlled by an omnipotent and personal being that is directly involved with every detail of life, from the color in the flower that Buddha picked to the affairs of the heart of man. This God who created the universe, and all that is in it, revealed himself to the world in these writings, and then in the form of the God-man Jesus Christ. Jesus Christ made claims of deity about himself, and then proved his deity by his death and bodily resurrection from the grave in the presence of many credible witnesses. Jesus Christ claimed to be "the way, the truth and the life" (John 14:6). He "breathed on" His disciples and said, "Receive the Holy Spirit" (John 20:22). He did not say, "Breath in the ki." The Bible states that from his throne flow the "rivers of the water of life" (Revelation 22:1).

If these teachings are truth, then the concepts of dualism symbolized in the Tae Guek are false, as is the ki, because the omnipotent God is the ultimate force that controls the fate of the universe. In fact, the Bible teaches that God is light and there is no darkness in him. There is not an equal opposite. In his pride, Satan, an angel God created and gave a free will, tried to proclaim himself equal with God. The pride of Satan led to his expulsion from the presence of God (Isaiah 14:12-15). By virtue of God's plan for mankind, this fallen being was exiled to earth for a period of time prior to the Great Judgment. Bitter because of his banishment, this once beautiful angel became the epitome of evil, and to this day, he seeks to separate men from God through all kinds of deceptions and false teachings (Mark 13:22-23).

Because of these facts, the religious tenets of Buddhism, Hinduism, traditional taekwondo and other Eastern martial arts are irreconcilable with the teachings of the truth revealed by Jesus Christ. However, the Bible teaches that Jesus Christ is a God of mercy and compassion, virtues to which every martial arts student and warrior should aspire. Because of His great mercy, this God of love is slow to anger and quick to forgive those who recognize their inability to live up to the standards of holiness required to enter into His presence. Instead of judging them according to their merits, God chooses to empower them through their own weakness, in order to reveal Himself as a God who cares about those that He created.

When God created men and women, He made them marvelously complex and complicated, and included a free will in their nature so that they could know and understand love. That will also has a tremendous potential for creative ability and accomplishment. Learning to focus the will to accomplish a task is the objective of the student of Christian martial arts. The kiap, in reality, is simply a method of focusing the power of the will. The proper execution of the kiap is a complete focus of the will and a burst of human energy released at the moment the physical body strikes the real or imaginary object. This action is accompanied by a guttural expression that emanates from the diaphragm. The effect is not a sound, such as the yelling of the phonetic enunciation of "kiap," but rather a highly efficient transfer of the energy developed in the physical movement directed by the student. The audible sound of the kiap is more similar to the grunt a man makes when lifting a heavy object. The student must stay focused on the objective to properly complete the movement.

Even though the kiap may have been characterized through false religious teaching, the Bible teaches that what the evil one intended for harm, God can turn into good. Because Jesus Christ is a God of mercy, when He exercises His grace, men are no longer bound by the legalistic aspects of the law. God no longer holds against men simple physical acts or words that are not conducted in idolatry or disobedience to His commands. The Bible teaches, "For physical training is of some value, but godliness has value for all things" (I Timothy 4:8). God recognizes man's need for physical exercise and accomplishment, and is willing to help the man or woman that seeks the truth about every area of life. When the student of Christian martial arts looks to the ultimate and wise God for every need, the student's will becomes properly focused. Then he or she understands the Holy Scripture: "I can do all things through Christ which strengtheneth me" (Philippians 4:13 KJV).

Reconciling the Kiap to Christ

Olympic boxers

An Organic Christian Defense

An organic Christian defense is possible with any type or form of fighting, from hand-to-hand combat to dogfights in the sky. Taekwondo, one the most popular and fastest growing forms of fighting in the world, is a physical and a mental discipline, with a practical application to protect one's self or others from harm. With an emphasis on kicks and punches, taekwondo is well suited as a competition sport, in which two combatants engage in full contact sparring in a match controlled by rules and referees. In a self-defense or defense of others situation, all control is up to the student, and the lives of everyone involved may very well depend on the outcome. In this case, the mental aspects of any martial arts system play a far larger role than the hand and foot techniques or weapons because the physical aspects become reflexive. For the Christian martial arts student, in addition to the physical components, the proper understanding and application of the mental and spiritual training must be mastered in advance, to achieve the best outcome. As an example, the five tenets of taekwondo are highly effective for self-defense if they are understood and enhanced with a Christian perspective.

Courtesy is the quality that allows the martial artist to avoid or defuse a confrontation before it ever reaches the stage of physical contact. The student of taekwondo is expected to always be polite to other people in every setting, and to avoid behavior that precipitates an altercation. Respect for others allows the student to maintain the high moral ground that is necessary to prevail in a confrontation. Although courtesy is similar to humility, it must not be confused with submission. Unless the student can simply walk away, he must be able to avoid any tendency to yield to an adversary, once the situation deteriorates beyond the hope for a civil resolution.

Integrity is the quality that gives the student of taekwondo the ability to recognize the point at which force may be required to resolve a confrontation. However, integrity is also the attribute that a student can use to avoid being caught in a situation in which the probability of violence is high. For example, a man or woman of integrity should not habitually attend public events or places where alcohol may be consumed in excess and fights are common. Nevertheless, circumstances sometimes put a student in harm's way, in which case the situation must be rapidly and accurately evaluated to determine the appropriate response. In other words, the actions of the student will be judged after the incident, and it is imperative that the decision to fight is justified.

Perseverance comes into the equation after the decision to fight is made. It is imperative that the student must be willing and able to continue the fight until it is safe to stop. Knowing when to stop fighting requires the student to be able to recognize the level of force necessary to subdue the opponent. For example, when confronted by a common bully, the student may be required to simply stand up to the aggression, which may even include an exchange of blows. However, a killer or a rapist intends great bodily harm, in which case lethal force may be required for survival. In either case, once the decision to fight is made, the student must persevere in the fight aggressively and without hesitation, until the adversary is dominated.

Self-control gives the student the edge necessary to gain an advantage over the opponent. The student must carefully control his or her actions until the appropriate point at which physical contact is initiated, once it is determined that force is necessary to resolve the conflict. If physical contact is delayed, the student must use self-control to overcome emotions that could adversely affect the outcome, such as paralyzing fear or trepidation. It is absolutely imperative that the student maintains his wits to gain the edge necessary to survive. The student has a limited amount of time in which to determine the appropriate course of action, with no second chance. More often than not, the winning edge is gained by the element of surprise. The element of surprise is accomplished by striking the adversary first, with great force to the most sensitive and convenient target. In hand-to-hand combat, the first strike must be followed up immediately with a persistent barrage of well-placed kicks and punches applied with force. The opponent must not be allowed to raise a defense, and must never be given a reprieve, or the opportunity to retaliate. At this point, the student will be fighting instinctively. Self-control allows the student to continue the attack until safe, and to stop fighting at the appropriate point without inflicting unnecessary bodily harm to the adversary. However, the student absolutely must continue the attack until the opponent is incapacitated or unwilling to continue and a clear escape from danger can be accomplished.

The **indomitable spirit** of the student of taekwondo is the tenet that keeps the student alive in any circumstance, even in the face of death. In the direst situation such as kidnap or war, a student of fighting may become captive to a hostile enemy and may be subjected to extreme physical abuse such as rape or torture. In this unfortunate situation, the indomitable spirit is the spark of life, the hope that an opportunity for escape or rescue is inevitable, even if it takes substantial time. In the more common self-defense situation, the student may have lost the initiative and be faced with sparring the adversary in an exchange of blows. Physical injury and pain are likely to be received, but the student must not give up the fight. The indomitable spirit of the student must be used to rejuvenate the other tenets of taekwondo, such as perseverance and self-control, to continue the battle until the opponent is overcome.

In conclusion, when a student begins to understand the five tenets of taekwondo, he gains a set of fighting principles to go with Christian life principles that are useful in every situation, whether it is living a peaceful life or facing great adversity, either natural or manmade. However, sooner or later every human gets to a situation in which he is utterly helpless, regardless of the strength of his body or will; for example, when facing eminent death. In all these cases, the student is best served with a broader understanding that includes the concept of an omnipotent God who controls the outcome of every situation. The student of faith will then learn that the most important tenets to survive, when all of his resources are exhausted, are taught in the Holy Bible with an organic understanding of Ephesians 6:13-18:

> Therefore put on the full armor of God, so that when the day of evil comes, you may be able to stand your ground, and after you have done everything, to stand. Stand firm then, with the belt of truth buckled around your waist, with the breastplate of righteousness in place, and with your feet fitted with the readiness that comes from the gospel of peace. In addition to all this, take up the shield of faith, with which you can extinguish all the flaming arrows of the evil one. Take the helmet of salvation and the sword of the spirit, which is the word of God. And pray in the spirit on all occasions with all kinds of prayers and requests. With this in mind, be alert and always keep on praying for all the saints.

Jael kills Sisera, captain of Canaan

The Political Spiritual Battle

God designed men to fight, just as women were designed to raise children. But God designed women to fight fiercely, and we recoil at the idea. Women fight fiercely because they are programmed to defend the home, yet certain groups want to send young mothers to the front lines. The Boy Scouts of America are vilified because they refuse to allow homosexual scoutmasters to sleep with their troops in pup tents in the woods. A general in the Pentagon is censured for speaking about morality among soldiers.[1] Meanwhile, the Church ordains homosexual priests, and politicians try to force the military to allow open homosexuals within the ranks. In the City of Brotherly Love, Christians arrested for preaching at a gay pride festival are charged under "hate crime" laws.[2] People are arrested and castigated for speaking the contents of their hearts and accused of crimes because the listener does not agree. Those who stand on principle are acridly and vehemently called "hatemongers" and become victims of the very crime for which they are charged. The world is upside down.

Nothing has really changed. About 2,700 years ago, the prophet Isaiah spoke about God's people:

The vineyard of the LORD Almighty is the house of Israel, and the men of Judah are the garden of his delight. And he looked for justice, but saw bloodshed; for righteousness, but heard cries of distress. (Isaiah 5:7)

His words describe the world today:

Woe to those who call evil good and good evil, who put darkness for light and light for darkness, who put bitter for sweet and sweet for bitter. (Isaiah 5:20)

As lawmakers make laws that punish the intent of the heart over the character of the crime, so man reflects the value God places on the relationship among human beings. As is the value of men to God, so is the value of the law, because He desires justice. In Old Testament times, God provided cities of refuge for murderers if the sin was not committed in malice (Numbers 35). But since Jesus Christ came and died on the cross and rose from the grave, the laws of man have gone through a steady metamorphosis. The Church grew among nations that rose and fell at the whim of God. The influence of the Church on culture was important for developing laws and rules of civility,[3] not unlike the codes of conduct in traditional martial arts. But there remained other deeper concepts common to man such as courage and honor. In "The Abolition of Man," C.S. Lewis wrote of the values of the natural law, which he referred to as the Tao.[4]

In western civilization, the natural law was embodied in chivalry, the qualities of medieval knighthood, which included bravery, courtesy, honor, and protection of the weak, especially women. The qualities of chivalry live in the heart of the Christian warrior, but the battle is against him. Since Christ ascended, the spiritual battle on earth has heated up and the enemy has advanced his lines. The enemy is inside the Church and government and he is eating away at the territory of God. The Church has split and run at the onslaught, and lost its influence in the affairs of men. However, there are solid Christians who recognize the battle for what it is and fight in the political arena to stand up for virtue. For example, the Boy Scouts should be commended for their gallantry. But they are just one troop in a battle of a large war.

The world bristles at the Christian warrior because it fears him and it hates him. And so the rulers, authorities, and powers of this dark world marshal their evil forces against the Christian and all that he stands for. Indeed it is the rage of Satan at his impending doom, having realized his inability to hold Christ in the grave. The Devil's attack is insidious and cruel. It is the rising tide that floods the land. The Church stands defenseless and alone apart from the mercy of God.

The metaphor stands as the persecution of the Church continues unabated in spite of its growth over two millennia. The critics apply fresh coats of the paint of the Inquisition, while the disciples of Marx are absolved of the blood let by Stalin, Mao Tse-Tung, Pol Pot, and others. Expunged from the schools in America in the name of the separation of church and state, Christianity is hypocritically replaced with the religions of secular humanism,[5] transcendental meditation, and yoga. In Moscow, thugs storm the sanctuary to beat parishioners, and police attack Christians demonstrating at the loss of their building permit.[6] In China, the Church meets in basements to whisper worship, as its pastors sit in prisons. The media never points out the Christian and Jewish effigies in the jihadist's training videos. The training is put to use in church bombings in Pakistan. In Australia, Christian pastors are arrested for proselytizing Muslims.[7] The Church in America lives in a shrinking bubble, and the Church in the world lives in peril. And no one comes to its rescue.

And who would? Nobody rescued Abel! The government will not rescue the Church, because the government is like the king who kills the children that threaten his throne. A democracy will not rescue the Church. Indeed, the greatest democracy in history betrayed the Church in Iraq when it toppled a ruthless dictator (perhaps righteously, perhaps providentially), then installed an Islamic constitution in the heart of civilization, where the extent of diversity justifies the tolerance and protection so cherished by modern society. But perhaps the motive was not so noble if democracy, or those who would manipulate it, simply desired the dictator's throne. Democracy without checks and balances is capable of great oppression; many innocent men have been hanged at the popular verdict.

To be fair, the government's fear of usurpation is not limited to its perceived threat from the Church. As the government seeks to drown her, it drowns everything around her. Just as Satan did not recognize God in Jesus Christ, so the government cannot distinguish absolute truth. But rather than grant all liberty and show mercy, it seeks to enslave all it can control and destroy all that it cannot. For example, since the Communists gained power in China in 1951, the Chinese people must be in the state-controlled Chinese Patriotic Catholic Association to worship legally,[8] and the popular Falun Gong religious movement is suppressed alongside the independent Christian churches. The Buddhist Dalai Lama of Tibet has lived in exile in India since the Chinese occupation in 1959.[9]

In comparison, in pluralistic America, the Bureau of Alcohol, Tobacco and Firearms (BATF) confronted a heretical, pseudo-Christian cult near Waco, Texas, suspected of federal firearms violations. After a botched raid, a 51-day siege began that culminated in an attack ordered by the United States Attorney General. On April 19, 1993, with training and equipment provided by the National Guard, agents led by the Federal Bureau of Investigation (FBI) attacked the compound, which led to its destruction by fire and the death of 76 people, including 26 children. That day, the BATF raised its flag over the Branch Davidian compound. The President of the United States said he would not accept the resignation offer of the Attorney General simply "because some religious fanatics murdered themselves."[10]

Interestingly enough, after the retaliatory bombing of the federal building in Oklahoma City, the FBI went on to publish methods for assessing the threat from militia groups within the country. The FBI profile of the most likely militia member describes "white males who range in age from the early 20s to the mid 50s. The majority of militia members appear to be attracted to the movement because of gun control issues…[believe] that the government is becoming more tyrannical and attempting to reverse constitutional guarantees…generally maintain strong Christian beliefs and justify their actions by claiming to be ardent defenders of the Constitution [sic]."[11] These ignoble and antique qualities are combined with paranoia of government conspiracies to define four levels of threat. These threat levels are used by the FBI to decide whether to call the militia up on the telephone and ask its representatives what they are up to, or run a wiretap and conduct covert operations. At least the capricious bureaucrats recognize the value of communication.

And so the governments grow without the influence of the Church. It is imperative that the Church train men and women who will serve in government positions such as police, military leaders, rulers, and politicians. In democracies, the Church must persuade with the value of its teachings to develop the loyalty inside government to support the ideals that provide for justice. In kingdoms, the anointed rulers must personally submit to God, support the Church, and govern with humility of heart and accurate scales. The despots must be brought down, and the liberty must be provided to preach the message that calls men to peace.

The Apostle Paul encouraged the new believer to "submit himself to the governing authorities, for there is no authority except which God has established" (Romans 13:1). But responding to orders from the Sanhedrin not to speak out about Jesus, the Disciples Peter and John said, "Judge for yourselves whether it is right in God's sight to obey you rather than to obey God. For we cannot help speaking about what we have seen and heard" (Acts 4:19-20). Subsequently, they were reminded in prayer of King David's song, "Why do the nations conspire and the peoples plot in vain? The kings of the earth take their stand and the rulers gather together against the LORD and against his Anointed One" (Psalm 2:1-2). Then the Holy Spirit shook the room (Acts 4:31).

Jesus Christ explained it all:

> If the world hates you, keep in mind that it hated me first. If you belong to the world, it would love you as its own. As it is, you do not belong to the world, but I have chosen you out of the world. That is why the world hates you. Remember the words I spoke to you, 'No servant is greater than his master.' If they persecuted me, they will persecute you also. If they obeyed my teaching, they would obey yours also. They will treat you this way because of my name, for they do not know the One who sent me. If I had not come and spoken to them, they would not be guilty of sin. Now, however, they have no excuse for their sin. He who hates me, hates my father as well. If I had not done among them what no one else did, they would not be guilty of sin. But now they

have seen these miracles, and yet they have hated both me and my Father. But this was to fulfill what is written in their Law: 'They hated me without reason.' (John 15:18-25)

The Political Spiritual Battle

A government and its subjects

As-salaam Alaykum

"Peace be upon you."

This is the standard "Hello" in the Arabic Middle East. After the conversation is over and the agreement is struck, the two men part with "Insha'Allah," the will of Allah, or let the will of Allah be done. When the deal falls through because one of the men failed to show up, he flatly states it was not Allah's will. Allah caused him to oversleep.

On September 11, 2001, radical Islamic fundamentalists flew jet planes full of passengers into buildings in America, killing more than 3,000 innocent people in one of the most successful acts of terrorism in history. But it was only one incident in a string of attacks in and on various nations and cultures during the past 40 years, ranging from the murder of Jewish athletes at the Munich Olympics, to the assassination of Egyptian president Anwar Sadat, to the destruction of ancient stone Buddha carvings in Afghanistan. The President of the United States stood up and said radical Islamic terrorists had hijacked the "religion of peace."

The expression of Islam bears its message. Its boys are sent to madrassas (schools) where they are indoctrinated into the Koran and its religious rituals, as strict monitors watch the children closely to keep their noggins bobbing. The madrassas of Pakistan and Afghanistan are known for their militancy, historically funded by Islamabad, Saudi

Arabia, and believe it or not, Washington, D.C.[1] The curriculum includes teaching hatred for America and Israel, and Christians and Jews.

Girls study from behind a see-through mirror,[2] if they are allowed to study at all. Sequestered in the home, the women of Islam are hidden behind veils in public and forced to ride in the back of the pickup truck with the goats.[3] In the name of honor, a teenage girl is stoned for falling in love with a boy in another sect.[4] The Taliban shoot the winsome maidens in the head at halftime in the futball stadium. (If there were any political will in the world with the value of a pound of salt, some nation would have invaded Afghanistan just to rescue the women, just as David rescued Keilah from the Philistines.) In Holland, an Islamic Moroccan stabbed Theo Van Gogh, the famous artist's nephew, in the chest because he produced a short film about the oppression of women in Islam.[5]

The Islamic government of Sudan sponsors the "Janjaweed" to commit genocide on the tribes of Darfur. Car bombs and human bombs murder without discretion from Israel to Lebanon to Paraguay. In Saudi Arabia, the muttawa, the religious police of the Commission for the Promotion of Virtue and Prevention of Vice, under the authority of "Sharia law," use canes to enforce dietary rules, dress codes, segregation by sex, business closures during the five prayer calls blasted from loud speakers each day, and mosque attendance.[6] In Mecca, the pilgrims circumambulate the Kaaba as if it were a mill. The children of Ishmael are enslaved.

As a matter of fact, the Islamic religion has spread around the world since Muhammed galloped on camelback across the sands of Arabia, approximately 600 years after Jesus Christ rose from the grave. Its adherents cross racial and cultural lines much like Christianity; they include Islamic Arabs, Persians, Mongols, Turks, Indonesians, Filipinos, Africans, Caucasians, and numerous other groups. To be fair, most of the Muslims in the world live at peace, and most likely wish to be left alone, as most people do. But the Arabs are of particular interest because they are the race of the prophet Muhammad, the founder of the religion of Islam, and they claim to be descendants of Ishmael, the first son of Abraham.[7]

This claim is not without dispute;[8] however, the actual lineage of the Arabs is beside the point. The point to be made here is that both the Muslims and the Jews trace their ancestry to Abraham, whose offspring would be as numerous as the stars (Genesis 15:5). For the sake of this argument, let us assume that the lineage is correct or, at least, that a large number of the descendants of Ishmael are Arab Muslims in the Middle East.

The providence of God is not something to take lightly, and a study of Abraham's family is important to know God. As inferred, both the Arabs and the Jews trace their heritage to him. But the Arab's heritage is one not of religion, but of the world. God promised to make Abraham "into a great nation...I will bless those who bless you, and whoever curses you I will curse; and all peoples of the earth will be blessed through you" (Genesis 12:2-3). But Abraham and his wife, Sarah, became rather old and had not had a son, so Sarah had this big idea, like, you know, for Abraham to sleep with her Egyptian handmaiden. After Hagar conceived, Sarah resented her, and ran her off into the desert. So God sent the angel of the LORD to look for Hagar there, and found her and comforted her. And he said to her:

> Go back to your mistress and submit to her...I will so increase your descendants that they will be too numerous to count...You are now with child and you will have a son. You shall name him Ishmael, for the LORD has heard of your misery. He will be a wild donkey of a man; his hand will be against everyone and everyone's hand against him, and he will live in hostility toward all his brothers. (Genesis 16:9-12)

In light of this passage, it is difficult to blame Islam for the clash between the Sunnis and the Shiites in Iraq, the location of Ur, the home of Abraham. But the Islamic nations bring the curse of God upon themselves when they curse Israel (Genesis 27:29). As the story goes, Sarah went on to conceive and bore Isaac, at the ripe old age of 90. Isaac was the father of Jacob and Esau, and Jacob, renamed, became the father of the twelve tribes of Israel. This is what God said to Abraham about his sons:

> You will call him Isaac. I will establish my covenant with him as an everlasting covenant for his descendants after him. And as for

> Ishmael, I have heard you; I will surely bless him; I will make him fruitful and greatly increase his numbers. He will be the father of twelve rulers, and I will make him into a great nation. But my covenant I will establish with Isaac whom Sarah will bear to you by this time next year. (Genesis 17:19-21)

It is often said that Ishmael was the child of the flesh, and Isaac was the child of the promise. And so the world tolerates Islam because the world and the flesh and Islam have a lot in common. Consider Colossians 2:20-23:

> Why...do you submit to [the world's] rules: "Do not handle! Do not taste! Do not touch!"? These...are based on human commands and teachings. Such regulations have an appearance of wisdom, with their self-imposed worship, their false humility and their harsh treatment of the body, but they lack any value in restraining sensual indulgence.

The world and Islam hate Judaism and Christianity because the former are of the flesh and the latter are of the spirit, and the flesh and the spirit are in battle. For completeness sake, it must be noted that Jesus Christ was a descendent of Judah, one of Isaac's twelve grandsons. It is in the Jews that the purpose of God has been shown in deed and in prophecy throughout the history of man, and it is in

Jesus, that "all peoples on earth will be blessed through [Abraham]" (Genesis 12:3).

In 2002, an open letter to the American people attributed to Islamic terrorist Osama Bin Laden was widely distributed in the media. In his self-righteous tone, Bin Laden excoriates America for its liberty and all the vices that go along with it. He justifies his destruction for the cause of piety, and pronounces judgment and doom upon everyone outside of the Islamic faith. Some would say it sounds just like Christianity. But there is a key and fundamental difference, as different as Allah and the great "I Am" (the LORD). Conversion to Islam is mandatory under that religion. There is no free will. Without a free will, there can be no love. Islam enslaves its adherents and converts because Islam is their master.

In sharp contrast, the Christian is humble, and he recognizes his sin committed in the liberty of the soul, which has the volition to choose between right and wrong. He knows he is helpless in the strength of his flesh, and in his flesh there is nothing inherently good, except the Holy Spirit of God that lives within him. The Holy Spirit of God came in, only upon invitation, as a guest who knocks at the door. The Christian knows Jesus is a man of peace and a friend, one who you can know and love, just like a man can know his neighbor, just like a boy can know his father. Indeed, in Jesus is Father Abraham, the father of many nations. Paul the Apostle, citizen of Rome and a complete Jew, said to the Galatians:

> You are all sons of God through faith in Christ
> Jesus, for all of you who were baptized into
> Christ have clothed yourself with Christ. There
> is neither Jew nor Greek, slave nor free, male
> nor female, for you are all one in Christ Jesus.
> If you belong to Christ, then you are
> Abraham's seed, and heirs according to the
> promise. (Galatians 3:26-29)

It is here that the Christian is bound up with the Jew
and the Arab, because in Jesus, the brothers and sons of
Ishmael and Isaac are brought together on an equal basis, as
servants to a true master servant who leads with the
righteousness of Jesus Christ. The Jew is the child of the
promise, and the promise was fulfilled in Christ. Together,
they incur the wrath of the world. The wrath is displayed in
Islam, and the twelve tribes each of Ishmael and Isaac and
their descendants are caught up in the violence of the curse
of God. It is only in the blessing of Jesus Christ promised
to all men that any one can truly be free.

The Church has no beef with Islam. It just wants to be
free to worship God, share His love with people, and
preach the Gospel to anyone who will listen. And for this,
the Church is marked for blood, and its converts from Islam
are beheaded. The radical Islamic fanatics may be a small
percentage of the whole, but they are the ones who declared
war on the Church, and they are not sleeping in. The
Church may recognize its enemies, but it is ill prepared to
fight, tucked under its security blanket in the West and
fully exposed everywhere else. The world looks for its

enemies, but it doesn't know how to discern, so it mows over everything in its path. And so the planet steams along, with the smog of violence that God tried to quench in the Great Flood still belching forth across the skies. Everyone is caught up in it, from the grass huts to the mansions, from the monasteries to the mosques, from the halls of Parliament to the chambers of Congress. The enemies of the Church need to know that her children will not go undefended against the edge of their swords.

As-salaam Alaykum

Rebuilding the walls of Jerusalem

Broken Walls

and

Broken Laws

As it now stands, not much has changed since the Crusades, except instead of the Catholic influenced monarchies fighting the Muslims and whomever, the mostly secular governments have fought each other several times and now the fight is back with the Muslims. But Bin Laden's minions call the current global war a Crusade.

Their jihad is in response to their belief that the powers of the world and the power of the Church and the Synagogue are the same thing. But apart from the Vatican, and the original benefit of the rise of free nations like the United States of America, there is no government power on this planet fighting specifically for the Church. The Christian warriors motivated by such ideals as chivalry, who exist within the ranks of the military, religious, and political offices of the world, serve this cause. The Christian warrior leaders are few and far between, and their expression is suppressed.

These noble and common men and women volunteer due to the call in their hearts, within the system that is available to them. They often appear as chess pieces used by those who rule from the high places. It is noteworthy that the First Crusade was more like a grassroots revival, and was the only Crusade that rescued Jerusalem and foreshadowed its destiny, bloody as it was from the friction of war. But as the Second and subsequent Crusades may have been misfires shot from cannons lit by political artillerists, within the ranks and population apparently were Christian warriors, physical and spiritual.

Certainly imperfect like most of God's people, Richard the Lionhearted was respected enough for his military prowess that Saladin negotiated a truce with him and gave him ground on the coast to provide access for pilgrims to reach Jerusalem, short lived as it may have been.[1] But as King Solomon taught, a warrior is not the highest calling (Proverbs 16:32) (although God's gifts are not mutually exclusive). In the fifth crusade, Saint Francis of Assisi, a man of peace, walked into the tent of the Sultan of Egypt.[2] What if al-Kamil had converted? What if Franklin Graham could preach in Kabul Stadium?

Religious bloodshed, civil wars, regional and world wars, aspiring global conquerors that periodically rose up and rode out in arms—such events continued over the centuries. But recently it seems that the defending armies are limited in their ability to fight, not by the logistics of large armies or the friction of war, but by foolish political leaders who are not warriors and do not understand how to fight. They send the military out in high technology to put up their dukes and spar. But that is the way to get hurt in a fight, not the way to win; there is no time-out bell in war. And so the enemy, not bound by the rules of the match, jumps out of the ring and attacks the crowd. It took three jetliners slamming into buildings before Tom Burnett and Todd Beamer and others rolled out of their seats to fight back. The heroes are out there, but the leadership seems hard to come by. Christian warrior leadership training must be included in the role of the Church. Without it, the redoubt of liberty is in ruins.

It is not the intent of this review to assign blame or justification for conquests, or argue the virtue of the Crusades or jihad, but rather to point out that there are serious threats against the Church and the liberty of souls, and that their fate is bound up with the governments and religions of men. But until Christ comes again, the Church remains a part of, or subject to, the governments that come and go in various forms around the world.

If the Church will not train men and women to lead and to fight, then either the governments or the world will, for their own purposes. Those governments and entities that do not fight will be assimilated by those who do. If the Church will not lead the fight for justice, in spirit and deed, then nobody will. If the Church will not fight to save souls, then nobody will. If the Church will not fight to save the innocent and the oppressed, it will find itself under the curse of God.

Man has a tendency to try and justify his actions, especially in his sin. Indeed this study is intended as an apologetic for the men and women within the Church who hear and answer the warrior's call, as an appeal to those warriors outside of the Church who misunderstand the nature of God, and as an effort to reach those children and teenagers hemorrhaging out of the doors of the Church (as well as those who never enter in).

There can be no doubt that many will grab onto these arguments to justify their own violent bias against other groups. It is important to be clear that the purpose of this study is not to justify those abominable and reprehensible groups like the Aryan Nations, the Ku Klux Klan, al-Qa'ida, and the like, or those who would bomb abortion clinics or marketplaces and indiscriminately commit murder. Nor is its purpose to justify the blood previously shed by the Church in the name of religion. Perhaps it is the failure of the Church to teach the warrior attribute of God that has contributed to the trigger-happy tendency of those who would slay the so-called infidel for his unbelief. There can be no worse cause for murder.

This study used analogies, mostly from the Old Testament, to show that God used warriors for divine purposes over history. But the role of God's warriors in New Testament history becomes subjective, because the Scriptures are complete, and the correlation of scriptural prophecy with relatively recent, recorded history is pretty much esoteric. But from a layman's perspective, assuming that God has not changed, and the nature of man has not changed, there is little evidence to assume that God's use of prophets and warriors would change either. The main difference now is that God has revealed His spiritual parallel with the children of Abraham, and those children are the believers of Christ within the Church. The parallel extends between the Church and Jerusalem. If the Church is "the Holy City, the new Jerusalem, coming down out of heaven from God, prepared as a bride beautifully dressed for her husband" (Revelation 21:2), then one must consider the current condition of that town.

Just as children need fences, boundaries not only to protect them, but also to constrain their behavior as they grow, so the Church needs its walls. Even the New Jerusalem of heaven has marvelous walls (Revelation 21:9-21). Currently, the walls of the Church are broken down and its inhabitants are vulnerable, similar to Jerusalem in the fifth century B. C. under King Artaxerxes of Persia. When Nehemiah began to rebuild the walls, the politicians criticized him:

> But when Sanballat the Horonite, Tobiah the Ammonite official and Geshem the Arab heard about it, they mocked and ridiculed us. "What is this you are doing?" they asked. "Are you rebelling against the king?"

> I [Nehemiah] answered them by saying, "The God of heaven will give us success. We his servants will start rebuilding, but as for you, you have no share in Jerusalem or any claim or historic right to it." (Nehemiah 2:19-20)

The Church must follow the example of Nehemiah, who posted an armed guard as he rebuilt the crumbling walls of Jerusalem while he managed the doubting Jews and Arabs and the political powers that tried to thwart his efforts (Nehemiah 4). As it stands, Christian warriors are scattered and with few leaders, fighting to survive in a world that is against them. But the battle is getting closer to home. The curse of Ishmael's animosity toward his family is spreading around the world, and with it comes the chains and swords of Islam. The conquest of Jerusalem is the goal.

Hear the words Nehemiah told his people:

> Don't be afraid of them. Remember the Lord, who is great and awesome, and fight for your brothers, your sons and your daughters, your wives and your homes...The work is extensive and spread out, and we are widely separated from each other along the wall. Wherever you hear the sound of the trumpet, join us there. Our God will fight for us! (Nehemiah 4:14-20)

The United States government was wrong not to protect Christians in Iraq with a secular or neutral constitution, because in Christians in the Middle East is the brotherhood of the spiritual sons of Abraham. The Muslims have no historical claim to the area, or the people, that is any more legitimate. Governments must allow for open debate in the arena of ideas, and the various religions must accept the consequences of the strength of their arguments. The Mormons and the Freemasons are deceived by their occult religions. The Hindus are lost in a sea of gods with no consistency. The Buddhists are lost in the ethereal self.

The Islamic religion is mechanical and legalistic; within it there is no liberty or salvation by grace. Like the Muslims, the Jews are under the curse of the law, blind to their own Messiah. As Paul pointed out to the Galatians:

> After beginning with the Spirit, are you now trying to attain your goal by human effort? Have you suffered so much for nothing—if it really was for nothing? Does God give you his Spirit and work miracles among you because you observe the law, or because you believe what you heard?
>
> Consider Abraham: "He believed God, and it was credited to him as righteousness." Understand then, that those who believe are children of Abraham. The Scripture foresaw that God would justify the Gentiles by faith, and announced the gospel in advance to Abraham: "All nations will be blessed through you." So those who have faith are blessed along with Abraham, the man of faith.
>
> All who rely on observing the law are under a curse, for it is written: "Cursed is everyone who does not continue to do everything written in the Book of the Law." Clearly no one justified before God by the law, because, "The righteous will live by faith."…Christ redeemed us from the curse of the law by becoming a

curse for us, for it is written: "Cursed is everyone who is hung on a tree." He redeemed us in order that the blessing given to Abraham might come to the Gentiles through Christ Jesus, so that by faith we might receive the promise of the Spirit. (Galatians 3:3-14)

The other numerous religions and cults in the world all miss the mark. In truth, all mankind falls short, which is why Jesus Christ came, to fulfill the Law (Matthew 5:17-20). No one else could do it. The Christian warrior, as much as anyone, can live at peace with all these souls, but his mission is to speak the truth in love. He understands the Servant-Master who calls men to serve freely, and he does not force others to follow his faith through the imposition and enforcement of laws. There can be no salvation at the point of a sword. The Christian warrior strives to live a life of peace and of love for God and fellow man, and to fulfill the Law as best as possible in this fashion.

Let no debt remain outstanding, except the continuing debt to love one another, for he who loves his fellowman has fulfilled the law. Love does no harm to its neighbor. Therefore love is the fulfillment of the law. (Romans 13:8-10)

It is the love of God that moves the Christian warrior. He does not look for opportunities to attack his enemy or to get revenge. Rather, he prays for his enemy and seeks to overcome evil with good. He heeds the advice of Paul, "As far as it depends on you, live at peace with everyone" (Romans 12:17-21). The Christian warrior knows that it is the love of God shown through Christians that brings about free will conversion to faith in Jesus Christ.

The Christian mission is to save souls. It is a sin for a Christian not to rescue a damsel in distress; it is a sin for a Christian not to stop the killer in his tracks; it is a sin for the Christian not to go to war against the genocide of innocent souls; it is a sin for the Christian not to love the Arab or the Persian or the Jew, the religious or the irreligious.

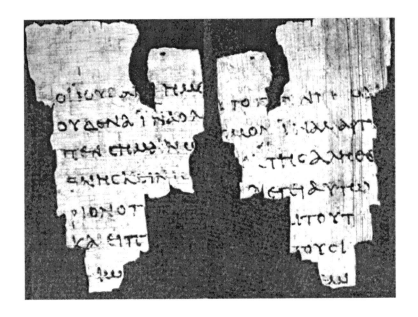

The Living Word
"Sharper than a two-edged sword"

The Prince of Peace

Through the ages, God has appeared to man and spoke to woman in various ways; but in each encounter, God was always consistent in His identity and purpose. God has wrestled with man and battled with him regardless of the man's stature or affiliation. God always controlled the outcome by His righteous justice and His divine purpose. To say that Jesus Christ is not a fighting man is to deny the Holy Scriptures. In fact, He is a king over a great army. God speaks to this from one of the oldest fragments of New Testament scripture extant from approximately 150 A. D.[1] From a tiny scrap of paper, Jesus Christ speaks with Pilate, the Roman governor, of the appropriate time to fight for His kingdom:

> Pilate…asked him, "Are you the king of the Jews?"
>
> "Is that your own idea," Jesus asked, "Or did others talk to you about me?"
>
> "Am I a Jew?" Pilate replied. "It was your people and your chief priests who handed you over to me. What is it you have done?"

Jesus said, "My kingdom is not of this world. If it were, <u>my servants would fight</u> [emphasis added] to prevent my arrest by the Jews. But now, my kingdom is from another place."

"You are a king then!" said Pilate.

Jesus answered, "You are right in saying I am a king. In fact, for this reason I was born, and for this I came into the world, to testify to the truth. Everyone on the side of truth listens to me."

"What is truth?" Pilate asked. (John 18:33-38)

Those who blame the Jews for the murder of Jesus are blind fools. Jesus was betrayed by the world in God's divine plan for the redemption of mankind. He paid the sacrifice of a warrior when He did what was necessary to bring down the pillars of sin that enslave His people. Like Samson, He pushed apart the barriers that confine men when He died on the cross at Calvary. And like Elijah and the other heroes of the faith over the ages, God's image and the image He created in man has been sawn in two, tramped down, beaten, and run over by a world that seeks to master and enslave all that it can control. But God is the liberator of the oppressed and His ultimate purpose will be fulfilled.

The Christian master warrior and martial artist understand the example that Christ set as a servant of charity, and so they love peace. The next time we all together see Jesus Christ, He will be recognized in a flash because the Prince of Peace will ride in on a white horse dressed for battle. He will appear on earth with a vast army because He knows that there can be no peace until evil is vanquished into the pit. The prophet Isaiah speaks of God and His mission of peace:

> The people walking in darkness have seen a great light; on those living in the land of the shadow of death a light has dawned. You have enlarged the nation and increased their joy; they rejoice before you as a people rejoice at the harvest, as men rejoice when dividing the plunder.

> For as in the day of Midian's defeat, you have shattered the yoke that burdens them, the bar across their shoulders, the rod of their oppressor. Every warrior's boot used in battle and every garment rolled in blood will be destined for burning, will be fuel for the fire.

> For unto us a child is born, to us a son is given, and the government will be on his shoulders. And he will be called Wonderful Counselor, Mighty God, Everlasting Father, Prince of Peace.

> Of the increase of his government and peace there will be no end. He will reign on David's throne and over his kingdom, establishing it and upholding it with justice and righteousness from

that time on and forever. The zeal of the LORD
Almighty will accomplish this. (Isaiah 9:2-7)

The kingdoms and democracies and tyrannies of the
world will be brought down because Jesus Christ will carry
the responsibility of rule with authority. The governments
intuitively know this and so they seek to kill the Church,
just as King Herod sought to kill Jesus as a child (Matthew
2:7-18). Righteousness will prevail and Jesus Himself will
establish His kingdom, and at His feet every knee will bow
and tongue will confess that Jesus Christ is Lord (Isaiah
45:23, Philippians 2:10-11). At that time, there will be
judgment, and all things will be called to account. But God
is merciful, so He provided a way to absolve man of his
guilt, and He offered it freely to those who would accept
His precious gift of forgiveness that leads to eternal life.
The servant's heart of a warrior made the ultimate sacrifice
to liberate man from the bondage of sin. Then He rose from
the grave to signal the defeat of death and evil. There will
be a time when God will open the gates of heaven and all
things will be new. Then, and only then, will there be
peace, and the bloodshed will be over.

Until that time, the Church must train men and women
to be ready when the battles come. They must not fight as a
catalyst to Christ's return, because God said, "Woe…to
those who say, 'Let God hurry, let him hasten his work so
we may see it'" (Isaiah 5:18-19). The righteousness of
Jesus Christ must be the Christian warrior's guide in every
decision of life and death. But if the Church sits back and

waits for the slaughter it is at risk of the wrath of God. God cursed the Israelites who ignored the warrior's call.

> "Curse Meroz" said the angel of the LORD, "Curse its people bitterly, Because they did not come to help the LORD, to help the LORD against the mighty."(Judges 5:23)

The Church must train to fight in spirit and in truth. The Church must enter the battle to save souls. It is her purpose. God has made it clear.

He is not hidden in the shadows. He is not an assembly of ideas or a universal Godhead. He is the great I Am. He is the Holy Trinity, the litmus test for all religions. He is the Way and the Truth and the Life, and the Name unto which men and women have access to God (John 14:6). He is active in the lives of men and women and intent upon His purpose. He is calling men and women unto Himself, and revealing Himself as a master warrior teacher.

> They will make war against the Lamb, but the Lamb will overcome them because he is the Lord of lords and the King of kings—and with him will be his called, chosen and faithful followers. (Revelation 17:14)

He loves each one of us enough to come to our rescue, and lead the fight against the forces of evil that seek to devour and enslave our lives. He teaches us how to live among others in peace and prosperity. He teaches us how to enter the battle when it is required, and He fights on our behalf when we depend on Him.

> The LORD will fight for you; you need only to be still. (Exodus 14:14)

Jesus Christ guarantees the victory. "Victory in Jesus" is our song. The shofar is sounding.

Holy Father,
Grant me a repentant heart, forgive me of my
sins, and cover me in your blood.

Teach me to be a righteous warrior, tempered
by justice, and motivated by your love.

In Jesus name. Amen.

Notes

The references to World Wide Web addresses were current as of the copyright date, and the citations reflect the address to the reference material at that time.

Chapter 1—Introduction
1. The story of the life of David is told in the First and Second books of the prophet Samuel, Chapters 1 & 2 of First Kings, and First Chronicles.

Chapter 2—Christian Martial Arts Defined
1. Taekwondo is often pronounced as three distinct syllables, and occurs in various writings as Tae Kwon Do, Taekwondo and taekwondo. The same sort of inconsistency occurs with the transliterations to English for other traditional martial art names. This book adopted the use of taekwondo to refer to the sport or martial art in general, except in reference to the Christian martial art of "Christian Taekwondo". The other traditional martial arts and related transliterations are referenced without elaboration.
2. From http://ailab.kyungpook.ac.kr/kmd/korea_music.htm; a form of traditional, native Korean music.
3. From http://www.japan-guide.com/e/e2113.html; a form of traditional Japanese music used in ancient courts.
4. From notes of the author taken during lessons from a respected Christian teacher. The use of the teacher's material in no way implies his endorsement of the ideas presented herein.

Chapter 4—Martial Training in the Bible

1. From http://www.blueletterbible.org; the English transliteration of the Hebrew word for "trained" is "chaniyk" and is referenced as Strong's Concordance entry number 02596.
2. From http://www.blueletterbible.org; the English transliteration of the Hebrew word for "armed" is "ruwq" and is referenced as Strong's Concordance entry number 07324.
3. "Enter The Dragon? Wrestling with the Martial Arts Phenomenon" by Erwin de Castro, B. J. Oropeza and Ron Rhodes, Christian Research Institute, (not dated) http://home.earthlink.net/~ronrhodes/Martial1.html.
4. From http://www.blueletterbible.org; the English transliteration of the Hebrew word for "teach" is "yarah" and is referenced as Strong's Concordance entry number 03384.

Chapter 5—The Sound of the Shofar

1. From "The Modern Significance of Taekwondo as Sport and Martial Art: Overcoming Cultural and Historical Limitations in Traditional Thinking" by Dr. Steven D. Capener, Ewha Women's University, Dept. of Korean Studies, published in *Coach Identification and Development Program, Level 1- Introducing Sport Taekwondo Manual*, 1st Edition, USA Taekwondo (not dated).
2. The English transliteration of the Hebrew word for "valiant men" is "chayil " (phonetically pronounced "khah-yil") and is referenced as Strong's Concordance entry number 02428. The Hebrew Lexicon definition includes "strength, power, might (especially warlike, valour) [sic]…" From http://www.blueletterbible.org.

Chapter 6—Warriors of the Faith

1. This is one of many scriptures which uses the "unutterable" name of God referred to as the Tetragrammaton, "YHVH," translated as LORD, a detailed review of which can be found at http://www.hebrew4christians.com/Names_of_G-/names_of_g-d.html.
2. Footnote to Judges 11:30-31, *The Life Application Study Bible*, Zondervan, 1991.

Chapter 7—Learning from the Warriors of God

1. "Types of Christ" by Paul Mizzi at http://www.monergism.com/thethreshold/articles/topic/Hermeneutics.html.
2. Introduction to Exodus, "Themes and Theology," *The NIV Study Bible*, Zondervan, 1985.
3. Footnote to Exodus 17:11, *The NIV Study Bible*, Zondervan, 1985.
4. Footnote to Exodus 17:9, *The NIV Study Bible*, Zondervan, 1985.
5. Footnote to Numbers 13:16, *The NIV Study Bible*, Zondervan, 1985.
6. Introduction to Joshua, "The Life of Joshua," *The NIV Study Bible*, Zondervan, 1985.

Chapter 9—The Warriors Refreshment

1. From notes of the author taken during lessons from a respected Christian teacher. The use of the teacher's material in no way implies his endorsement of the ideas presented herein.
2. Ibid.
3. Ibid.
4. From notes of the author from the *Full Flame Film Series*, Christ For All Nations, 2006.

Chapter 10—The Need

1. From http://www.olympic.org/uk/sports/index_uk.asp

Chapter 11—The Authority to Fight

1. Footnote to Luke 22:36, *Life Application Study Bible*, Tyndale House, 1991.
2. "Enter the Dragon? Wrestling with the Martial Arts Phenomenon" by Erwin de Castro, B. J. Oropeza and Ron Rhodes, Christian Research Institute, (not dated) http:////home.earthlink.net/~ronrhodes/Martial1.html.
3. Articles by Hollander, et. al., *Anchorage Daily News*, October 29, 2003 and April 15, 2005.
4. "Securing the Faithful," *Christianity Today*, February 1, 2008, http://www.christianitytoday.com/ct/2008/february/16.21.html.
5. "Guard's hands 'didn't even shake' as she shot gunman" by Electa Draper, *The Denver Post*, December 24, 2007.
6. From http://www.courttv.com/news/2007/1211/colorado_shootings_ap.html.
7. From http://www.timesonline.co.uk/tol/news/world/africa/article3117310.ece.

Chapter 12—One Long Blast

1. From http://www.olympic.org/uk/games/ancient/events_uk.asp.
2. From http://en.wikipedia.org/wiki/Pankration.
3. For examples, see //www.bullshido.net.
4. "Enter the Dragon? Wrestling with the Martial Arts Phenomenon" by Erwin de Castro, B. J. Oropeza and Ron Rhodes, Christian Research Institute, (not dated) http://home.earthlink.net/~ronrhodes/Martial1.html.
5. From notes of the author taken during lessons from a respected Christian teacher. The use of the teacher's material in no way implies his endorsement of the ideas presented herein.
6. *The Screwtape Letters* by C. S. Lewis, MacMillan Publishing Company, New York, N. Y., 1961.

Chapter 13—A Model for Discipleship

1. From "The Modern Significance of Taekwondo as Sport and Martial Art: Overcoming Cultural and Historical Limitations in Traditional Thinking" by Dr. Steven D. Capener, Ewha Women's University, Dept. of Korean Studies, published in *Coach Identification and Development Program, Level 1-Introducing Sport Taekwondo Manual*, 1st Edition, USA Taekwondo (not dated).
2. See //www.kukkiwon.or.kr/english/information/information01.jsp?div=01 for more information.
3. *Tae Kwon Do* by Yong Chin Pak, Iowa State University, 1996
4. Ibid.

Chapter 14—Reconciling the Kiap to Christ

1. *Tae Kwon Do* by Yeon Hee Park, Yeon Hwan Park, and Jon Gerrad; Facts on File, Inc., New York, New York, 1989.
2. *Yoga: Bob Larson Speaks Out* by Bob Larson; Bob Larson Ministries, Denver, Colorado, 1986.
3. *Tae Kwon Do* by Yong Chin Pak; Iowa State, Ames, Iowa, 1991.
4. *Understanding the Times* by Dr. David Noebel, Harvest House, Eugene, Oregon, 1991.

Chapter 16—The Political Spiritual Battle

1. "Conservatives Rally Around General Pace" by Nathan Burchfiel, Cybercast News Service, March 15, 2007, //www.cnsnews.com/ViewNation.asp?Page=/Nation/archive/200703/NAT20070315e.html.
2. "Christians Arrested While Preaching At Gay-Pride Event" by Adrienne S. Gaines, *Charisma*, 2007, http://www.charismamag.com/display.php?id=10626.
3. *George Washington's Rules of Civility* by John T. Phillips, II, Goose Creek Productions, Leesburg, Virginia, 2005.

4. *The Abolition of Man* by C. S. Lewis, Harper Collins, San Francisco, CA, 1944.

5. *Understanding the Times* by Dr. David Noebel, Harvest House, Eugene, Oregon, 1991.

6. "Evangelical Christians Fight for a Church" by Stephen Boykewich, *Moscow Times*, Issue 3185, June 10, 2005.

7. "Pastors' convictions for quoting Quran overturned, Case was brought under version of 'hate crimes' legislation", *World Net Daily*, December 28, 2006, //www.wnd.com/news/article.asp?ARTICLE_ID=53526.

8. "Fu Tieshan, Head of China's State Church" [dies], Associated Press, *The Boston Globe*, April 22, 2007.

9. From http://www.friends-of-tibet.org.nz/dlama.html.

10. "No Confidence: An Unofficial Account of the Waco Incident" by Timothy Lynch, Cato Institute, April 10, 2001, http://www.apologeticsindex.org/pa395.pdf.

11. "Militias: Initiating Contact" by James E. Duffy and Alan C. Brantley, M.A., FBI, 1997, http//www.fbi.gov/publications /leb/1997/july975.htm.

Chapter 17—As-salaam Alaykum

1. "Mastering the Madrassas" by Anwar Iqbal, United Press International, *Washington Times*, 2003, http://www.washtimes.com/world/20030817-123032-5826r.htm.

2. According to http://www.shariahprogram.ca/arabic-grammar-faqs.shtml#teachingsisters.

3. Based on personal observations of the author.

4. "The moment a teenaged girl was stoned to death for loving the wrong boy," *Daily Mail*, London, England, May 3, 2007, http://www.dailymail.co.uk.

5. From
http://en.wikipedia.org/wiki/Theo_van_Gogh_(film_director)
6. This information is well known, but for an interesting
perspective on the religious police visit
http://muttawa.blogspot.com/.
7. From http://www.answering-
christianity.com/ishmael_great_nation.htm.
8. According to http://www.bible.ca/islam/islam-myths-arabs-
descendants-of-ishmael.htm.

Chapter 18—Broken Walls and Broken Laws
1. *A Concise History of the Crusades* by Thomas F. Madden,
Rowman & Littlefield Publishers, Inc., 1999.
2. Ibid.

Chapter 19—The Prince of Peace
1. The original fragment shown here is located at the Rylands
Library, Manchester, England.

Chuck Cobb is available for speaking engagements and personal appearances. For more information contact:

Chuck Cobb
C/O Advantage Books
P.O. Box 160847
Altamonte Springs, Florida   32716

To purchase additional copies of this book go to:
www.toknowawarrior.com

or call our toll free order number at:
1-888-383-3110 (Book Orders Only)

or visit our bookstore website at:
www.advbookstore.com

Longwood, Florida, USA
"we bring dreams to life"™
www.advbooks.com